AN HUMBLE SUPPLICATION TO HER MAIESTIE

AN
HUMBLE SUPPLICATION
TO HER MAIESTIE

BY

ROBERT SOUTHWELL

EDITED BY

R. C. BALD

CAMBRIDGE
AT THE UNIVERSITY PRESS
1953

PUBLISHED BY
THE SYNDICS OF THE CAMBRIDGE UNIVERSITY PRESS

London Office: Bentley House, N.W. 1
American Branch: New York

Agents for Canada, India, and Pakistan: Macmillan

Printed in Great Britain at the University Press, Cambridge
(Brooke Crutchley, University Printer)

PREFACE

The editing of this small prose work has proved a far more exacting task than the one originally planned. At first nothing more was envisaged than a reprint of the rare and little-known octavo, but as the manuscripts came to light the deficiencies of the printed text soon became apparent, and editing on a more elaborate scale had to be undertaken. If the labours of collation and of preparing a critical apparatus have sometimes seemed excessive, the editor has at least the satisfaction of offering a reasonably correct text of a work which deserves more attention than it has ever received.

For various kinds of help freely given the editor tenders his grateful thanks to the Rev. Leo Hicks, S. J., the Rev. J. H. McDonald, C.S.C., Professor W. A. Jackson, Professor Ernest Strathmann, and Dr G. H. Russell. The authorities of the Honorable Society of the Inner Temple and of the Henry E. Huntington Museum and Art Gallery have generously permitted full use of the manuscripts in their possession; and it would be ungracious indeed for the editor not to acknowledge his debt to the John Simon Guggenheim Memorial Foundation, the Huntington Library, and the Faculty Research Committee of Cornell University for assistance which enabled the work of editing to be carried through to its conclusion.

CONTENTS

CONTENTS

INTRODUCTION

I

Elizabethan enactments against the Catholics came in waves, and were invariably related to political events, either at home or abroad. The first group of recusancy laws in 1571 was a direct result of the Rising in the North and the papal bull of excommunication against Elizabeth. A decade later, Spanish successes in the Netherlands, the presence of papal forces in Ireland, and the coincidental arrival of the first Jesuit mission to England stimulated a new series of statutes and proclamations against the Catholics. Then, in 1584, further Spanish successes, coupled with the assassination of the Prince of Orange, inevitably brought about a fresh reaction in England; men of all classes bound themselves together by the Oath of Association for the protection of the Queen and, when Parliament met at the end of the year, two more bills against the Catholics were immediately introduced and passed. Three years afterwards yet another anti-Catholic bill became law, this time under the impending threat of the Spanish Armada.

Though the danger of a Spanish invasion was successfully averted in 1588, the defeat of the Armada by no means marked the end of Spanish power. In 1591 the situation in the Netherlands was still precarious, and there was further danger yet nearer home; a combined force of Spaniards and Leaguers had established themselves in Normandy, from which they were trying to expel Henri IV. Elizabeth was quick to realize that the Spaniards had almost within their grasp bases from which an invasion would be far more feasible than it had been in 1588, and there were already rumours that a fresh Armada was in preparation. English forces were despatched to the aid of the Protestant allies with less hesitation than had been shown at any other time during Elizabeth's reign, and, as an obvious corollary, new measures to repress the Catholics at home were proposed. There was no Parliament sitting, so the government had recourse to a proclamation issued by the Queen in Council.

The proclamation[1] is dated 18 October 1591, but it was apparently not issued until late in November.[2] By comparison with some of

[1] See Appendix I.
[2] There is some doubt as to the actual date of its publication. Persons refers to it as 'promulgatum Londini 29 Novemb. 1591', and Stapleton as

the earlier enactments, the regulations now established were not particularly stringent. In order 'to withstand & prouide speedy remedy against the...fraudulent attempts of the Seminaries, Iesuites, and Traitors', commissioners were to be appointed in every shire, city, and port to search out and examine all persons suspected of having had communication with those beyond the seas, and house-holders were to be called on, if necessary, to supply full particulars of all who had dwelt in their houses at any time during the past year. But more galling to the Catholics than the regulations them-selves were the violence and intemperance of the language of the proclamation. The Pope was a 'Milanois vassaile' of Spain; the seminarists were 'a multitude of dissolute yong men who [had] partly for lack of liuing, partly for crimes committed become Fugitiues Rebelles and Traitors'. These 'vnnatural subiects of our kingdom, (but yet very base of birth)', 'these venomous vipers' had been to Rome and Spain to be 'instructed in Schoole pointes of sedition', and from thence had returned to infect the realm. The proclamation, in fact, relied for its effect less on its regulations than on its propaganda.

The Catholic exiles were not slow to take up the challenge. The most notorious reply came from the pen of the most powerful of all the Catholic writers, the Jesuit Robert Persons, who far outdid the proclamation in scurrility in his *Elizabethæ Angliæ Reginæ... sævissimum in Catholicos sui regni edictum...cum responsione ad singula capita* (1592). Persons's book also circulated in an abbreviated version in English made by some of his colleagues, under the title *An Advertisement written to a Secretarie of my L. Treasurers in Ingland* (1592). Three other books of the same tenour, all dated 1592, came from the Catholic presses abroad: John Cresswell's *Exemplar Literarum missarum e Germania ad D. Guilielmum Cecilium*, Thomas Stapleton's *Apologia pro Rege Catholico Philippo II...contra varias & falsas Accusationes Elisabethæ Angliæ Reginæ per edictum suum 18 Octobris datum*, and Richard Verstegan's *A Declaration of the true Causes of the great Troubles*.[1] But the violence of these replies did more harm than good, and their only result was to provoke still

'20 Novembris Londini proclamatum'. This discrepancy is probably due in part to the difference between the Julian and Gregorian calendars, but a more modern annalist, G. B. Harrison (*Elizabethan Journals*, I, 74), dates it 21 November, probably on the authority of Strype.

[1] For a brief account of these works and a discussion of their authorship, see Ernest A. Strathmann, 'Ralegh and the Catholic Polemists', *Huntington Library Quarterly*, viii (1944–45), 337–358.

severer legislation against the Catholics at the next meeting of Parliament.

The intransigents abroad were beyond the reach of persecution; the real sufferers were the Catholics at home. But they had already found their spokesman. Southwell's *Humble Supplication to her Maiestie* was written during the weeks immediately succeeding the issue of the proclamation, and its tone is in striking contrast to that of the protests which came from beyond the seas.

Robert Southwell, after ten years' preparation at Douay and Rome, had returned to England as a member of the Jesuit mission in 1586. In 1591 he was thirty years old, and for the past five years had endured all the dangers of his calling. His headquarters were usually in London, where he had found a secure refuge at Arundel House under the protection of the Countess of Arundel, whose husband was a prisoner in the Tower for his religion. Southwell was almost certainly in London towards the end of 1591; he must have heard of the proclamation as soon as it was issued and have begun his reply to it almost immediately. The allusion in it to 'the last Arraignement of three Priests at Westminster, even since this Proclamation', refers to the trials of Edmund Jennings, Eustachius White, and Polydore Plasden on 4 December; they were executed on 10 December, and the fact that Southwell makes no mention of their execution suggests that they were still alive while this passage was written. One textual tradition, which seems to represent the first draft of the *Supplication*, dates it at the end December 14; another, which is probably based on a fair copy into which some revisions had been incorporated, is dated 'This last of December'.[1]

Though the *Supplication* is in the form of a petition addressed to Elizabeth, Southwell, when he wrote it, had no hope that it could be presented to the Queen. He is said to have operated a secret press, so he probably intended to print it and thus put it into circulation.

We are forced [he wrote] to divulge our Petitions, and by many mouthes to open vnto your Highnes our humble suites. For neither daring our selues to present them in person, being terrified with the president of his Imprisonment that last attempted it, nor having the favour of any such Patron, as would be willing to make himself Mediator to your Maiestie, we are forced to committ it to the multitude, hoping that among soe many as shall pervse this short and true Relation of our troubles, god will touch some mercifull heart to let your Highnes vnderstand th'extremity of them.

[1] See below, pp. 31, 47–49.

In spite of this explicit statement of the author's intentions, a memorial submitted to the Pope some years later affirmed that the *Supplication* had been presented to Elizabeth: 'ad reginam Angliæ præteritis annis...a religioso quodam viro...exhibitus' and 'libellus iste supplex scriptus ac reginæ oblatus est.'[1] If Southwell still intended to put it into print, his plans for its dissemination were probably thwarted by his capture on 25 June 1592. On that day his active missionary life came to an end; there remained for him only imprisonment, torture, and the scaffold.

II

The after-history of the *Supplication* is curious. For some years it circulated in manuscript, and the few shreds of evidence suggest that copies were much prized. The memorial addressed to the Pope, which has already been cited, referes to it as 'libellus iste supplex...quem nos manuscriptum legimus', and the document to which this is a reply[2] states that, though it bears no declaration of authorship, 'patet tamen ex stilo et manuscripto[3] de quo diù mirifice gloriabantur Jesuitæ'. One early reader of whom we have definite knowledge was the Jesuit William Weston, who read the book in manuscript while he was a prisoner at Wisbech.[4] Somewhat later, about the year 1594, a copy fell into the hands of the notorious Topcliffe, who lent it to Bacon. In a letter to his brother Anthony, Bacon expressed his grudging admiration of the work, and suggested that it was worth transcribing. Bacon's letter is undated,[5] but it seems to belong to the time when he took part with Topcliffe in the examination of Henry Walpole, a Jesuit and fellow-prisoner with Southwell in the Tower. It is just possible, too, that Topcliffe's copy was the original of the transcript formerly belonging to Sir Thomas Egerton, which has survived among the Ellesmere manuscripts.

The *Supplication* was eventually published in 1600, not so much to appeal for sympathy for the Catholics as to embarrass the Jesuits. It was used as a weapon in the archpriest controversy, of which a brief account must now be given.

[1] See Appendix II (*b*).
[2] See Appendix II (*a*)
[3] Presumably an autograph manuscript.
[4] J. Morris, *The Troubles of our Catholic Forefathers*, II, 182.
[5] J. Spedding, *Letters and Life of Bacon*, II, 368.

Open strife between the Jesuits and the seminary priests (or seculars) first broke out in 1595 in Wisbech Castle, where a large number of priests were confined, and rapidly spread. It became so violent that in 1598 George Blackwell was appointed archpriest, in the hope that the institution of an office carrying authority over all the Catholic clergy in England would put an end to the quarrels. But Blackwell was instructed not to act without consulting the superior of the Jesuits, so that his appointment had every appearance of a victory for one of the contending factions; and, in any case, Blackwell was by temperament unfitted to heal the breach. Some of the secular priests soon questioned the validity of his appointment, since it had been made not by papal breve but merely by letters from the Cardinal Protector of England. Blackwell's authority had eventually to be confirmed by the Pope, and only then did those who had previously challenged it make their submission. With singular want of tact Blackwell immediately proceeded to accuse his late opponents of schism, and when some of them protested he suspended them. Their only recourse was an appeal to Rome. A petition, dated 17 November 1600 from Wisbech, was drawn up, signed by thirty of the leading priests, and despatched.[1]

Blackwell had previously been able to restrain his opponents from ventilating their grievances in print, but he could hold them back no longer. A flood of pamphlets came from the presses during 1601 and 1602. The quarrel was now public property; the authorities not only sought to fan the dissension, but secretly encouraged the appellants and connived at the printing of their books.[2] When a group of the appellants left for Rome in September 1601 to prosecute the appeal in person, they did so with official sanction.

The publication of Southwell's *Supplication* was the first shot fired in the pamphlet war. It appeared towards the end of 1600, falsely dated 1595, and appeared before the appellants had had time to compile and publish their accounts of their grievances. It is first heard of in a letter of 17 December 1600 addressed to Sir Robert Cecil by that very Robert Poley of whom Southwell writes so bitterly in his account of Babington's plot. Poley, now out of favour,

---

[1] For a full account of this controversy, with bibliographies of the pamphlets on both sides, see T. G. Law, *Jesuits and Seculars in the Reign of Elizabeth*, and J. H. Pollen, *The Institution of the Archpriest Blackwell*.

[2] See Gladys Jenkins, 'The Archpriest Controversy and the Printers, 1601–1603', *The Library*, 5th series, II (1947–48), 180–186.

was trying to reingratiate himself. He had managed to secure a copy of Southwell's book, and had evidently been so stung by its references to himself as to wish to reply, so he requested permission to write an exposure of the Jesuits. The passage referring to the *Supplication* is as follows:

The Booke inclosde was (as I thinke your Honor knowes) 5 years since disperste in wrytten Coppyes by the Author R. Suthwell. And lately by Garnet and Blackwell putt in printe though foreadvisde by good discretion nott to do itt. Wher the leafe is putt in your Honour maye readylye finde howe they deale with Sir Fra: Walsingham, I proteste most falcelye slandringe him and wyckedlye abusing him.[1]

But Garnet (the Jesuit superior) and Blackwell had had nothing to do with the publication of the *Supplication*; we have Garnet's word that the archpriest had, at his request, expressly forbidden it. In spite of the prohibition the book had been sent to press by John Boswell, one of the signatories of the appeal and an avowed opponent of the Jesuit faction. It was apparently printed in Staffordshire at a secret press worked by William Wrench and John Boulter, a former apprentice of John Danter; the distribution was looked after in London by a group consisting of Peter Bullock, bookbinder, and two Catholics who had already suffered imprisonment for their faith, James Duckett and John Collins. The Bishop of London was not only aware of the activities of this press but encouraged it, though in printing the *Supplication* it gave him more than he had bargained for.[2]

[1] Quoted by F. S. Boas, *Marlowe and his Circle*, pp. 115–116, and *Christopher Marlowe, a Biographical and Critical Study*, pp. 290–291.

[2] The story is told in 'The Information of William Jones Printer', presented to the Speaker of the House of Commons in 1604:

'John Boulter servant to John Dainter of London Printer was sent by the B. of London into Staffordshire and there he joined wth Will[m] Wrench in printing popish bookes and ther he contynued almost two yeares, vntill Wrench and he fell out about wages.

'In this tyme of Boulters being with Wrench was printed by them Traiterous bookes for w[ch] Wrench was condemned and obtayned his pardon by the B. of London his meanes as himself reporteth, though Bullocke the seller, Ducket and Collins the dispensers were executed.'

(H. R. Plomer, 'Bishop Bancroft and a Catholic Press', *The Library*, 2nd series, VII (1907), 174–175. Cf. also *Records of the Court of the Stationers' Company, 1576–1602*, ed. Greg and Boswell, pp. 58, 81.)

Duckett and Collins had both been in prison as recusants in 1593; their examinations are preserved in the Huntington Library in MSS. Ellesmere

It might be thought that the government would have connived at the publication of the *Supplication*, as they unquestionably did at the publication of the other books put out by the appellants. But Southwell's work was capable as none of the others were of winning sympathy for the Catholics, and, besides, no government could afford to allow Southwell's account of Babington's plot to obtain general currency. Accordingly the book was ruthlessly suppressed, probably as a result of Poley's letter to Cecil. The greater part of the edition was seized and destroyed; the books were found, one would guess, in the possession of Bullock. He was tried and condemned, but reprieved, and after lingering in prison for nearly a year turned informer. First Collins was taken, tried, and hanged; then Duckett was arrested. He was charged with the possession of twenty-five copies of the *Supplication*, but the jury refused to convict him on the sole testimony of Bullock and brought in a verdict of not guilty; whereupon the Chief Justice made them reconsider their verdict, reminding them that when he was arrested Duckett had had other Catholic books in his possession. Two days later, on 19 April 1602, Duckett was taken to Tyburn and hanged; at his side was Peter Bullock, whose treachery had availed him nothing.[1]

Meanwhile the little band of appellant priests had arrived in Rome. They knew well that they would meet with stiff opposition from the archpriest's party, which was headed in Rome by Persons, but they were prepared for a fight. Persons tried from the outset to influence opinion against them by circulating immediately after their arrival an 'Informatio de quibusdam Presbyteris qui nuper ex Anglia venerunt', but a copy soon fell into their hands. It contained a vigorous attack on their writings, charging them with heresy, and

---

2125 (3) and 3130 (2). Duckett is described as of St Dunstan's in the West, London, tailor, and Collins as of Winchester, mercer. Duckett admits that he had been engaged in smuggling Catholic service books and pictures over from Antwerp.

[1] A number of the facts concerning the publication of the *Supplication* are contained in two letters, one from Fr. Rivers and the other from Fr. Garnet to Persons. The relevant passages are printed in James H. McDonald, *The Poems and Prose Writings of Robert Southwell, S.J., a Bibliographical Study* (Roxburghe Club, 1937), pp. 117–118.

An account of Duckett's trial and execution was written by his son, who afterwards became Prior of the English Carthusians at Nieuport. It is printed in full in J. H. Pollen's *Records of the English Martyrs*, but was used earlier as the basis for the article on Duckett in Challoner's *Memoirs of the Missionary Priests*.

forewarning them that the orthodoxy of their publications would unquestionably be made an issue. It was an obvious piece of tactics to retaliate in kind. Soon afterwards (on 4 March 1602, the day before their first audience with the Pope) when they wrote to their friends in England they added a postscript: 'We pray you send us a copy of father Southwell's Supplication to the Queen.[1] Persons, who obviously had his methods of obtaining information, seems to have heard of their interest in Southwell's tract and to have written at once to Henry Garnet about it. Garnet's reply of 5 May is extant,[2] in which he relates the circumstances of its publication and promises to send a copy if he can find one. This, apparently, he was unable to do, though in due course a copy reached the appellants. Meanwhile in Rome the case had been proceeding step by step. At last, on 9 August, the judgement of a commission of six cardinals appointed by the Pope was communicated to both parties, and it contained, among other things a severe censure on the appellants' books. To this the appellants replied with a memorial to the Pope in which one of their requests was for a similar censure on the books of their Jesuit opponents.[3] In support of their application they presented on 22 August a number of objectionable passages, in Latin translation, from *Leicester's Commonwealth* (often attributed to Persons) and Southwell's *Supplication*. The Jesuits countered with a petition in defence of the *Supplication*.[4]

Persons affected nonchalance at the attempt of the appellants to discredit the books written on the Jesuit side, even though his own *Briefe Apologie*, written against the appellants, was among the books under attack:

they said [he wrote] that...some books also had as bad propositions: for proof whereof, they exhibited a certain supplication made, as is said, some years past, by father Southwell to her majesty, out of which book they alleged (as one cardinal himself related in my hearing) that he called the queen *clementissimam et supremam post Deum dominam*; which, belike, was, in our English tongue (for I have not read the thing itself) *most clement and sovereign lady under God;* which these now urged for heinous matter.[5]

[1] The letter is printed in *Dodd's Church History of England*, ed. M. J. Tierney, III, clv–clvi.

[2] See McDonald, *op. cit.* p. 118.

[3] T. G. Law, *The Archpriest Controversy*, II, 68.

[4] See Appendix II (*a*) and (*b*).

[5] Tierney-Dodd, III, clxxix.

As for the appellants, it cannot be denied that they hardly acted in good faith in making the use of the *Supplication* that they did. Their selection of 'offensive' passages was carefully chosen for those who were to see them. The first passage, for instance, was meant for the French Ambassador, who was to present the memorial on their behalf; most of the rest were torn from their context because of their courtly compliments to the excommunicated Queen (so that Persons's sneer was to some extent justified) or because they implied a denial of the more extreme claims of papal authority. With the real issues raised by the book and its relation to their own cause, they troubled themselves not at all.

In the end the Pope condemned all books written on either side of the controversy, and expressly forbade the publication of anything that might renew it.[1] With this judgement the *Supplication* faded into obscurity. It is mentioned in rather vague terms once or twice by Catholic historians of the succeeding centuries, but when Grosart edited Southwell's poems in 1872 he could find no trace of the book, and doubted its existence. Only recently has it received any attention at all; its rarity, added doubtless to the fact that the British Museum still catalogues it as an anonymous work, has prevented it from occupying the place in Elizabethan literature which it unquestionably deserves.

III

Southwell wrote the *Supplication* rapidly and vehemently. Few traces of his earlier euphuism remain; his prose has become more supple and more colloquial. His method of commenting on and refuting, phrase by phrase and section by section, the words of his opponent, is that of most of the controversial writers of the time. Even in the hands of so brilliant a controversialist as Persons this method is often unsatisfactory, while in a lesser writer such as the Anglican Thomas Morton it makes his work almost unbearably disjointed. Yet the *Supplication* possesses continuity and unity in an unusual degree. It is animated by the orator's passion. Southwell wrote of thoughts ever-present to his mind, and of things that were part of his daily experience. His sense of his mission, with its almost inevitable martyrdom, and his feeling for the sufferings of his fellow-Catholics were the impulses that prompted the work.

[1] Tierney-Dodd, III, clxxxii–iii.

Southwell's own experience is stamped on almost every page of his book. A youth of good family, he had left home at the age of fourteen to study at Douay, Paris, and Rome, and when he speaks of the seminaries, and of his companions and teachers there, he does so from first-hand knowledge. Allen and Persons, whom he defends, had been his masters and his friends. When he returned to England, he reached London a bare three weeks before the news of Babington's conspiracy became public, and it seems that an attempt was made to involve him in it.[1] During the active years of his mission, his movements were probably less restricted and his life less confined than some of his biographers have suggested. It is known that he visited Persons's aged mother at Nether Stowey to bring her aid and news of her son, and on another occasion he visited the captive priests at Wisbech. It seems likely too, on the evidence of the *Supplication*, that he had journeyed to the North of England at least once. On two occasions he is known to have taken refuge in the priest's hole while pursuivants searched the house in which he was hiding. Thus the sufferings he describes were ones which he himself had seen and shared.

There is also a prophetic quality in the *Supplication* which is not surprising.

The only fault [writes a historian] that can be found with the priests of the Elizabethan age is that their contempt for death often took the form of contempt for life and yearning for martyrdom. No worldling ever showed greater eagerness in the pursuit of worldly honour than they did in pursuing the 'crown' and the 'palm'. Their chief fear was that God would think them unworthy of this honour, and, in speaking of their brethren's martyrdoms, their words often ring with impatience to be following in their steps, and frequently it sounds as if they were often envious of their lot.[2]

The sense of impending martyrdom hangs over Southwell's pages. Even if he had never, though doubtless he had, been a spectator at a trial in Westminster Hall or among the crowd that thronged around the scaffold to administer some secret sign of consolation to the victim, he knew these things only too well from the lips of others, and had lived through them in imagination many times. 'The death

---

[1] J. H. Pollen, *Mary Queen of Scots and the Babington Plot* (Publications of the Scottish Historical Society, 3rd series, vol. III), pp. clxiii–iv.

[2] A. O. Meyer, *England and the Catholic Church under Queen Elizabeth*, p. 190.

of the martyrs remained the Catholic mission's most effective means for achieving its purpose',[1] and the missionaries were well aware that they must expect to suffer at any moment. Their martyrdoms, therefore, were achieved through years of preparation, and the *Supplication* shows how well Southwell had schooled himself to meet the fate that soon afterwards overtook him. The tortures, the trial under the statute which made him a traitor 'for religion only', and the cruel execution—all these he endured courageously and even high-spiritedly, secure not merely in his unshaken faith but in the knowledge that every gesture he made and every word he spoke might be the means to the conversion of some lost or doubting soul.

For this reason, then, the *Supplication* is a deeply moving work. In addition, one can admire Southwell's uncompromising firmness in all matters of religion. In affairs of state, on the other hand, he was prepared to concede the utmost to the royal power;[2] the distinction between the two was sharp and clear in his mind, and his

---

[1] Meyer, p. 212.

[2] He did not, however, go as far in this respect as his opponents would have wished. All his acknowledgements of the royal authority are most carefully worded, and even represent a qualification of it, as when he writes: 'we doe assure your Maiestie that what Army soever should come against you, we will rather yeald our brests to be broached by our Cuntrie swords, then vse our swords to th' effusion of our Cuntries bloud' (p. 35). Southwell does not say that he and his fellow-Catholics would take up arms against such an army, but only that they would rather be massacred than join it.

The examinations of recusants made in 1593, which are to be found among the Ellesmere MSS. in the Henry E. Huntington Library (nos. 2118–44), show that a question frequently asked of Catholic prisoners was: 'if the pope by his authority and th' aucthority of the Churche of Rome shall excomunycate the Quenes maiesty and thervppon pronounce her subiects to be freed of ther obedience and subiection to her maiesty, and then send an Army into this Realme to establishe that which he calleth the Catholicke Romysh religion, whether in the like case he will fight on the Quenes maiesties side against suche an Army or noe'. The perplexity and mental distress aroused by this question are apparent in a number of the answers to it. Southwell (p. 35, ll. 9–20) repudiates 'words alleaged of taking parte with an Army of the Popes against the Realme' in such answers as having been spoken either by priests under torture or by 'some vnskillfull Lay man, that not knowing how to answere such Captious questions, and for reverence of the Chiefe Pastor of gods Church, not daring to say he would fight against him, had rather venture his life by saying too much, then hazard his Conscience in not answering sufficient'. It may be doubted, however, whether Southwell's answer would have been deemed 'sufficient' by Topcliffe.

words bear a sense of his pride in being a loyal Englishman. South-well's return to his native country had stirred feelings long dormant in him, and he had come more and more to identify himself with the country and the spirit of its people. Yet in his appraisal of certain facts his judgement could not but be partial. Though a slowly widening gulf had separated him from the exiles on the Continent, many of the old ties still remained, and they were doubtless re-sponsible for his defence of Allen and Persons, for whom he always felt admiration and respect. Yet the temper and policies of these two men were essentially antagonistic to Southwell's. It is extremely unlikely that he had ever seen Allen's *Admonition to the Nobility and People of England and Ireland,*[1] and of course both Persons's reply to the proclamation and his *Conference on the next Succession* were still unwritten at the time of the composition of the *Supplication*. Such works as these, however, provided Elizabeth's government with ample justification for its anti-Catholic measures, even if it had possessed none before. Further, in spite of Southwell's denials, there is no question that certain English Catholics were prepared to serve in a papal army against Elizabeth, and lists of those who would rise against the Queen had been drawn up for the benefit of the Spaniards.[2] Again, though Southwell may have been technically correct in what he says about bulls, it was a fact that the bull of excommunication had absolved Elizabeth's subjects from their oath of allegiance and had inflicted penalties on those who obeyed her. It is true that Persons and Campion, at the time of their mission, had obtained a relaxation of its terms in so far as they applied to the English Catholics, but Allen's *Admonition* makes it clear that the full effect of the bull was to be revived as soon as the Spaniards landed in England. Even in his account of Babington's plot Southwell is not wholly reliable; he had, of course, only limited access to the facts. Poley and Gifford doubtless deserve the worst that can be said about them, but Walsingham's responsibility for the plot is a different matter. It was well known from an early date[3] that through his

[1] The *Admonition* was written to be circulated in order to prepare the English Catholics for the landing of the Armada, but Southwell's reference to Philip's 'first assault, when not any Priest or Catholique in *England* was acquainted with his coming, or sure of his intent, till the common voice bruited it, and our home provisions ascertained his purpose' (p. 36) makes it clear that he had no advance knowledge of the coming of the Armada.

[2] Such a document may be seen in Tierney-Dodd, III, xxviii–xxxi.

[3] E.g. see the account of the plot in Camden's *Elizabeth*.

spies Walsingham learned of almost every stage of the plot from its inception onwards and manipulated it for his own purposes; it cannot be questioned that he used it to press for the execution of Mary Queen of Scots, but that he originated it is not merely not proven but extremely doubtful.[1] Nor should sympathy for his victims blind us to the fact that even if Babington and his associates were dupes, living in a fantastic dream-world that had little relation to reality, they were still, by any definition of the term, traitors and deserved their fate.

Thus far, then, Southwell's statements cannot be accepted un-critically; but it is significant that some at least of his inaccuracies spring not from any lack but from an excess of patriotism: he had been sure from the first that his mission was wholly religious and in no sense political and was ready to 'render unto Caesar the things that are Caesar's' with the same fervour that he rendered to God the things that are God's. In one of his early reports to his superiors he characterized Babington's plot as 'that wicked and ill-fated con-spiracy, which did to the Catholic cause so great mischief',[2] and, discussing at Wisbech the prospects of a Spanish invasion, he declared 'that though the inuaders might, yet would they not spare one catholike in England, more then a protestant'.[3] Such statements are completely consistent with the attitude of the *Supplication*, and point the way to its true historical significance.

The archpriest controversy brought to a head a conflict within the ranks of the English Catholics which was far from being as narrowly legalistic as it appeared to be; it was a conflict between two conceptions of Catholicism. The point of view of which the Jesuits were the principal exponents was completely logical and rigidly uncompromising; it found its extreme expression in some of the writings of Persons. It maintained the papal supremacy in spiritual and secular affairs alike; the Queen was an excommunicated heretic, and therefore it was the duty of Catholics to bring about her over-throw in alliance with any Catholic force that might come against

[1] Conyers Read, *Mr Secretary Walsingham and the Policy of Queen Elizabeth*, III, 25–49, has given the fullest and least biased survey of the available evidence. J. H. Pollen's *Mary Queen of Scots and the Babington Plot* is in essence an attempt to justify Southwell's account of the plot, and Pollen's interpretation of the events has been largely followed in Alan Gordon Smith's *The Babington Plot*.

[2] 21 December, 1586, quoted by Pierre Janelle, *Robert Southwell the Writer*, p. 50.

[3] W. Watson, *A Decacordon of Ten Quodlibetical Questions* (1602), p. 177.

her. But the ordinary Catholic could not blind himself to the un-reality of such reasoning. He was on the horns of a dilemma; he wished to be at the same time a good Catholic and a good Englishman, but neither the Pope nor the Queen was willing to allow him to be both. Thus it was almost inevitable that there should emerge among many of the Catholics the opposing concept, parallel to the Gallicism of the French Church, of a national branch of the Catholic Church, theologically allied to the University of Paris and English in the same sense as that was French. Such a concept was far more capable of satisfying the emotional needs of the average English Catholic.

According to Meyer,[1] this view of English Catholicism was first given explicit statement by John Bishop in 1598, but it is already implicit in Southwell's *Supplication*, as the appellants were at pains to suggest in their memorial of 1602. Southwell's own feelings, no less than his experience in the mission, had taught him the vital necessity, if English Catholicism was to survive, of reconciling loyalty to Church and State. There is no question how far removed his position was not only from that of Allen and Persons but, one is forced to believe, from that of his fellow Jesuits in England. Thus it would seem that in what to us appears the noblest element in South-well's tract is to be found the very reason why, in the years immediately after Southwell's martyrdom, the *Supplication* was an embarrass-ment to his order; why it was put into print by their opponents; and why Henry Garnet, Southwell's superior, was satisfied to see in print the answers to the proclamation written by Persons, Stapleton, and Cresswell, but tried to suppress the *Supplication* itself.

[1] *Op. cit.* p. 420.

AN
HVMBLE
SVPPLICATION
TO HER MA-
IESTIE.

✠

Printed, *Anno Do.* 1595.

[Title-page of the octavo edition of 1600.]

NOTE

The present reprint is based on MS. Petyt 538.36 in the Library of the Inner Temple. This is the best of the surviving texts; not only are its readings in general superior to those of the others, but it carefully numbers each section of Southwell's reply, and italicizes his quotations from the proclamation—characteristics possessed by no other version.

No attempt has been made to furnish a facsimile reprint. Where they seemed necessary to the sense variant readings from the other texts have been introduced and the fact recorded in the Textual Notes; abbreviations (which are frequent) have been silently expanded; the numerals for each section appear at the beginning of the relevant paragraphs instead of alongside them in the margin. Otherwise the manuscript has been closely followed, even to idiosyncrasies of spelling (including its rather unusual treatment of *u* and *v*) and capitalization.

AN HUMBLE SUPPLICATION TO HER MAIESTIE IN ANSWERE TO THE LATE PROCLAMATION

Most mighty and most mercifull, most feared and best beloved Princesse: They are at the bottome of a helples misery, whom both a condemned estate maketh common obiects of abuse, and an vnpittied oppression barreth from discovering their griefes to those that are only able to afford them remedy: Every one trampleth vpon their ruines, whom a Princes disgrace hath once overthrowen, Soveraignes favours being the best foundations of subiects fortunes, and their dislikes the steepest downfalls to all vnhappines. Yet a Prince supplying the place, and resembling the person of All-mighty god, should be soe indifferent an Arbiter in all Causes, that 10 neither any greatnes should beare downe Iustice, nor any meanenesse be excluded from mercy. And therfore an humble Confidence in your Maiesties goodnes, perfect in all Princely vertues, and the only shoot-anker[1] of our last hopes, induced vs to lay open our manifold extremities, which hitherto (as it seemeth) haue bene scarcely heard, lesse believed, and nothing regarded. And though our Condition be soe desolate, that we can neither be freed from outward misery, but by becomming inwardly more miserable, nor Complaine of our troubles, but our very Complaints are punished:[2] yet an infamed life being to free mynds more yrkesome then an innocent death, we had 20 rather put our vttermost hazards to your Highnes Clemency, then seeme with our silence to giue credit to our obloquies: to which if we doe not, it may be imagined that we cannot answere.

There hath bene of late published, to our vndeserved reproach, soe strang a Proclamation, that it hath made your most affied[3] subiects doubtfull what to belieue, sith they see soe apparent and vncolourable vnthruths countenanced with soe reverend authority, and warranted with the most sacred title of their most honoured Queene. The due respect that eueryone carieth to your gratious person, acquitteth you in their knowledg from any meaning to 30

---

[1] *shoot-anker.* The earlier forms 'shoot-anchor' and 'shot-anchor' were not replaced by the more familiar 'sheet-anchor' until the seventeenth century.

[2] *our very Complaints are punished.* See note on p. 45, line 23 below.

[3] *affied.* Trusting, devoted.

haue falshood masked vnder the vaile of your Maiestie. Yet when they see your Soueraigne stile soe abused to th'authorizing of Fictions, that the Magistrates of your whole Realme, must generally soothe[1] things soe directly disproved by common sence, and contrary to their owne and all mens knowledg, it cannot but be a torment to their Christian mynds; yea, and it must needs make them iustly to scorne that any subiect should dare in soe high a degree to blemish both his Princesse and all her officers Creditts, as to draw them to averr his plaine and vnexcusable leasings. For
10 what can they thinke, but that this is either a racking of publique authority to private purposes, who not being yet ripe to reveale, their owne dangerous grounds, are forced to borrow these deluding shrowdes; or an open Condemnation of your Maiesties actions, as though they beare themselues vpon soe vniust and lawlesse motives, as could not able them for righteous, but by begging beliefe of these Counterfeit illusions.

We verily presume, that none of your Maiesties honorable Counsell would either shew soe little acquaintance with the Princes stile, as to deliver in your name, a discourse soe full farced with con-
20 tumelious termes, as better suted a Clamerous tongue, then your Highnes pen; or be soe slightly affected to the regard of your honor, as to defile it with the touch of so many false assertions: yet all men iustly marvaile that any Indytor durst adventure to disgorge their private ill will, rather then to observe decency in soe publique a thing: Yea they lament their owne Case, whome these abuses make vncertaine what to credit in serious points, importing their Cuntries and their owne safeties, when they see in this (which seemeth to be but a prologue to future tragedies) the strongest foundations to humane beliefe, applied in all mens mynds to sup-
30 port meere improbabilities. And though the Iniury offered to your Maiestie, and nearly concerning all your Realme, might in equity Challenge all mens penns to warne you of soe perilous Courses: yet sith Priests and Catholiques are the markes Chieflie shott at; we aske humbly leave of your Maiestie and Counsaile, to shew, how Chollerike the humor was towards vs, that cared not though the arrow hitt your Maiesties honor in the way, so the head thereof might enter into our hearts. It is an easy thing to be a true Prophet,

---

[1] *soothe*. 'To maintain or put forward a lie as being true', *O.E.D.*, which quotes from Savile's translation of Tacitus, 'Galba yielding to an vntruth so generally soothed, puts on a brest-plate'.

in foreseeing how this necessary Clearing of our selues wilbe aggravated to your Maiestie with heynous words, sith those that would dislodge vs out of all good opinions, will doubtles endeavour to fullfill any such Prophecie: But we now humble our Petitions to your Care of Innocency, that it may arme your eares against such partiall Appeachers, and incline you to measure your Censure with reason and Equity.

1. To make therfore our entrie with the vnfavourable termes, wherin we are often and generally called *vnnaturall Subiects*; we desire to haue it decided by your Maiesties owne Arbitrament, whether we haue iustly deserved to weare so base a Livery. If we live at home as Catholiques, professing our owne, and refusing to professe a Contrary Religion, we can neither keepe our places in the Vniuersity, nor follow our studies in the Innes of Court,[1] but we are imprisoned for Recusancy, impoverished, troubled and defamed. And yet if we leave all, and seeke free vse of our Conscience, and departe the Realme, taking such helpes as the Charity of other Cuntryes affordeth vs, we are straight reckoned for *vnnaturall Subiects*.

It is rather an *vnnaturall thing* to disobey the Author of nature for any Creature, in forsaking that Faith by which only we hope to be saved: And yet we must doe this, to the willfull murthering of our owne soules; or if we refuse it, be we at home or abroad, by these hard Censures we are proclaymed *vnnaturall*. All bonds and duties both of nature and grace, invite vs to loue god and our Cuntrie more then our lives, and our Neighbours as our selues, which if we observe in the highest degree, we hope, what other title soeuer we deserue, we shall at the least be deemed not to swarue very farr from the tenderest Rules of native Curtesie. We are vpon soe mighty and warrantable proofes assured by all Antiquity, that our Catholique Faith is the only truth (to which all that haue bene or shalbe saved must owe their fidelity) that we thinke it a worthier purchase, for the perseverance in the same, to forfeit our best fortunes, and engage our lives to the greatest Cruelties, then by revolting from it, to enter league with error, and to make our soules the price of infernall paine: If then, as we esteeme it at a higher rate then our owne lives, believing that out of it neither

---

[1] *neither keepe our places in the Vniuersity, nor follow our studies in the Innes of Court.* Because of the requirement of the Oath of Supremacy, imposed by the Statute 1 Eliz. c. 1.

god can be truly honoured, nor any soule saved; soe if we seeke
with our deepest perills to plant it in our Realme, and to winne
soules from misbeliefe vnto it, we thinke that we owe a most
sincere and *naturall* love vnto our Cuntrie: (for even by *Christs*
owne testimony, noe mans Charity reacheth to any higher point
then to yeald his life for the benefitt of his Friends.) And if others
that soe deeply touch vs for *vnnaturall* Creatures, would with as
much diligence haue searched out the truth by an indifferent tryall,
betwene the learned on both sides, as they haue with violence
10 martyred and oppressed vs, they would happily thinke themselues
more *vnnaturall*, for having misledd infinite soules into endles per-
dition, then vs, that with the sweat of our dearest bloud, seeke to
gleane a few scattered eares, the silly Reliques of their vnfortunate
harvest. And if our due Care of our Cuntry be such, that to reare
the least fallen soule among your Maiesties subiects from a fatall
lapse, we are contented to pay our lives for the ransome: how much
better should we thinke them bestowed, if soe a high a penny-
worth as your gratious self, or the whole Realme might be the
gayne of our deare purchase? But though they that hunt this fault
20 in vs, might best be their owne prey (our Faith being the strongest
ground of true and *naturall* fidelity) yet must we only be accounted
vnnaturall, being ballanced in their affections, that draw all Causes
of Compassion to Motives of Cruelty, and make their condemning
Reports the Commentaries of our dutifull meanings.

2. With the like spirit, still breathing more ill will then truth, he
termeth the Right honorable Lord *Cardinall* and Archbishop *Allen*,
and Father *Parsons* (both learned and reuerend men) *two seditious
heads*; looking happely through such eyes as Iudg all men to be
their owne Colours. And what Cause haue they given to this
30 slaunder, vnles it be accounted *Sedition* to gather the ruynes of gods
afflicted Church, and to haue provided Sanctuaries[1] for persecuted
and succourles soules, which forced at home either to live with
a goared Conscience, or to lie open to continuall vexations, rather
Chose to leave their Cuntry then their Catholique Religion. It was
noe *Sedition* for many in Queene *Maryes* tyme to be harboured in
Geneva, mayntained then by those that now enveigh against vs.
It is noe *Sedition* to admitt such multitudes of strangers as for their
Faith swarme into *England* out of all Cuntries. It is thought *Charity*
to ayde the States of *Flanders* in the behalf of Religion. It is extolled

---

[1] *Sanctuaries*. The English Colleges at Douay and Rome.

4

in your Maiestie as an honorable favour to protect the King of
Portugall[1] and Sir *Horacio Palavicino*.[2] But if we, whose Cause at
home in respect of our Faith is more lamentable then any Protestants in any other Cuntries, haue chosen two venerable men to
procure vs some refuge from our domesticall scourges, where we
may follow our studies, and exercise piety, strayte your Maiestie
(though induced to practise the same Courtesy towards others) is
informed against them as *Seditious heads*; soe true it is that the same
thing is not it self in divers persons. And yet (as god Almighty and
the world is our witnes) nothing in those *Seminaryes* is either [10]
intended or practised, but the reliefe and good education of such
forsaken men, as from the stormes of our English shoare flie thither
for a calmer Roade, till perfected in the Course of learning and
vertue, they may returne to offer their bloud for the recovery of
soules. And for the *basenes of their birth* (which among other like
points is interlaced, with as impertinent as scornefull a Parenthesis,
and a fitter note for this Penners then your Maiesties observation)
I meane not to dwell long vpon it: for the thing neither importeth
any offence to god, nor Cryme against your Maiestie, nor greatly
abaseth them, whom excellent vertues (the only true measures of [20]
worthines) haue ennobled: Yet this without disparagement to any
may truly be avowed, that the *Cardinalls Grace* is of as good and
auntient a house,[3] and euery way as worshipfully allied, as some of
the highest Counsellors were in their meaner fortunes, till your
Maiesties favour and their rare habilities made them stepps to
clymbe to their present honors. And whether of likelihood he
might haue carried as high a saile, if the tyme had equally seconded
him with as favourable gales, I leave to their Iudgments who are
privy to his present estate, greater then England can afford to any
Clergy man. For your Maiestie being as able to know, and noe [30]
lesse willing to vse the exellencies of your Subiects then other
Princes, it may be iustly presumed, that he might aswell haue
entered into Credit at home, if his Faith had not drawen his foote

---

[1] *the King of Portugall*. Don Antonio, a bastard nephew of the ill-fated
Don Sebastian, and the pretender to the throne of Portugal. He lived for
a time in England and received a pension from Elizabeth.

[2] *Sir Horacio Palavicino*. A financier, merchant and political agent of
Genoese descent who settled in England and was knighted by Elizabeth in
1587.

[3] *of as good and auntient a house*. William Allen was the second son of
John Allen of Rossall, Lancs., and Jane Lister of Westby, Yorks.

from the first stepp, as with strangers in a forrayne Cuntrie, where neither familiarity with the Peeres, nor acquaintance with the Prince, but the only fame of his worthines sent an admiration and love of him into their hearts. And whosoeuer considereth the manner of his advancement, being Created *Cardinall* alone, out of the ordinary tymes[1] (a prerogatiue seldome yealded but to spetiall persons) who marketh his wisdome to haue bene in such reverence, that in Pope *Gregories* the 14. his sicknes, he was thought the fittest among all the College of *Cardinalls* to be his Vicegerent in all spirituall Causes: who knoweth the small Cause that our Cuntrie (by Lawes, Libells, and all other meanes, seeking to vndermyne the Popes Sea) hath given him to reward her subiects with soe high promotions: Finally, who weigheth the endeavours of our Counsell to hinder his preferrment, and darken his vertues with hard Informations, shall easily belieue the man to be of rare and singuler perfections, that having noe other wings to beare vp his Credit, but learning and vertue, could reach to soe high points of favour, notwithstanding soe forcible and mightie letts. As for *Father Parsons*, he having placed the vttermost of his Ambition in Contempt of honor, and the highest of his wealth in voluntary povertie, will easily acknowledg his birth to haue bene of more honest then great Parents;[2] yet were they not soe meane but that they were able to

[1] *being Created Cardinall alone, out of the ordinary tymes.* At the special request of Philip II of Spain, who was then preparing for his attack on England, Allen was created a cardinal by Pope Sixtus V at a consistory held on 7 August 1587. His promotion is said to have caused considerable surprise, the more so because of a recent constitution of the Pope that no creation of cardinals should take place except in Advent.

[2] *his birth to haue bene of more honest then great Parents.* Persons was born at Nether Stowey, Somerset, the sixth of eleven children of a blacksmith. Southwell had visited his aged mother.

This passage is commented on in W. Watson's *Decacordon of Ten Quodlibeticall Questions concerning Religion and State* (1602), one of the more violent of the appellant tracts:

'I...greatly muse at the faire glosse of father *Southwell* concerning father *Parsons* birth and education. It being most vntrue that Fa. *Southwell* reports of him, scil. that hauing placed the vttermost of his ambition in the contempt of honor; and the highest of his wealth in voluntarie pouertie, will easily acknowledge his birth to haue bene of more honest then great parents. Yet were they not so meane, but that they were able to affoord him such education as might haue made his good parts a way to no small preferment, &c. All which is most false, a bastard he was; vnhonestly begot, basely borne, a *Wolsey* in ambition, a *Midas* in mundicitie, a traitor in action; which here

afforde him such education, as (if he had not raised his thoughts aboue all earthlie dignities) might haue made his good parts a way to no small preferment. And albeit his Credit be great with the King of Spaine,[1] (his vertue and rare wisdome deserving noe lesse) yet did he never vsurpe the title of *The Kings Confessor*, as this Inditor would perswade your Maiestie, though some of the simpler sort of our English soldiours in the gallies, vpon error and ignorance, muttered some such speeches among themselues. As for other Priests, how many of them are Knights and Esquiers Sonnes,[2] and otherwise allied both to worshipfull and noble houses, and heyres to faire Revenues, let their owne Friends and Parents dispersed through the whole Realme beare witnes! This only we may say in answere of our obiected *basenes*; that in the small nomber of the Catholique Priests of our Nation, (which reacheth not to the tenth of the Protestant Ministery) there are very neare as many, yea happily more gentlemen, then in all the other Clergy of the whole Realme.

3. Now wheras we are most vncurteously called, *a multitude of dissolute yong men*, we desire noe other evidence to disprove this accusation then an indifferent Censure. For first before our departure out of the Realme, we must resolue to abandon our Cuntrie, Frends, and all such Comforts as naturally all men seeke and finde in their natiue soile: we must relinquish all possibilities of favour, ritches, and Credit: we must limitt our myndes to the restrained and severe Course of *the Society of Jesus*, or the Semynaries; wher the place is in exile, the Rules strict, the gouernment austere, our wills broken, the least faults chastised, and a most absolute vertue exacted. And who can imagine those to be of soe *dissolute* humors, who thus determine to abridg themselues of all Causes of *dissolutenes*, and to

I had not touched, had he spared his owne Soueraigne and bloud royall of this land' (p. 108).

The charge of bastardy, so frequently brought against Persons by his enemies, was no new issue; it was first raised in 1574 when he was forced to resign his fellowship at Balliol.

[1] *albeit his Credit be great with the King of Spaine.* Persons went to Spain in 1588 and remained there for nine years. With the warm support of the King he established English seminaries at Valladolid, Seville and Madrid.

[2] *As for other Priests, how many of them are Knights and Esquiers Sonnes.* This claim, frequently made by the Catholics, that their clergy were drawn from a higher social stratum than those of their opponents, is abundantly justified. See H. R. Trevor-Roper, *William Laud*, pp. 27–29.

7

imprison their affections within the precinct of a Reguler and streight order? And least happely it may be imagined that we say more then in proofe we finde, it is knowne to thousands, and daily seene and witnessed by Travellers that we are there tied to soe precise termes in diet, aparrell, exercise, and all other things, that we are much more shortened of our scope then in any College of our English Vniuersities. I omit the Prayers, Fastings, hayre-Clothes, and other Chastisements of the body,[1] which being voluntary, yet vsuall, are to any (if not more then partiall Iudges) invincible grounds against this slaunder of our being *dissolute*. But let our entertaynement at our returnes be a finall ouerthrow of this false imposition. For who can thinke them *dissolute*, that being by the Lawes, by Examples, by comon experience taught, with what bloudy Conflicts they are here to encounter, and how many feares, dangers, and bloudy agonies both in life and death they are vndoubtedly to expect, are notwithstanding contented, for the reclayming of soules into gods fould, willingly to yeald their bodies to the hazard of all these miseries foreseene and foreknowne, and advisedly Chosen before all worldly Contentments.

But it may be that some vnacquainted with our estate, will measure our mynds by our apparell,[2] being (as we Confesse) more agreeable oftentimes to the common fashion, then to the graue attire that best suteth our Calling. Yet is neither our habitt, nor our behavior soe Ruffianlike or disordered, as this Inditor (euer forgetting truth when he remembreth vs) would haue it willingly imagined. But in this we must yeald our reason, sith we cannot reforme th'inconvenience till your Maiestie think it good to license

[1] *Prayers, Fastings, hayre-Clothes, and other Chastisements of the body.* Cf. Southwell's letter of October 1580 to John Deckers (*C.R.S.* v, 295–8), in which he speaks of his discovery of his vocation to enter the Society of Jesus: 'From that time our fervour in prayer began to increase; private chastisements of the flesh to afford delight; the unsparing use of the hairshirt and discipline to please exceedingly'.

[2] *our apparell.* On his arrival in England Southwell adopted the attire of a young gentleman of fashion (Pierre Janelle, *Robert Southwell the Writer*, p. 38). The elegance of the disguised Jesuit was often made a matter of reproach: 'If, about Bloomesbury or Holborne, thou meet a good smug fellow in a gold-laced suit, a cloke lined thorow with veluet, one that hath gold rings on his fingers, a watch in his pocket, which he will valew above 20 pounds, a very broad-laced band, a stiletto by his side, a man at his heeles,...then take heed of a Jesuit' (John Gee's *Foote out of the Snare*, 1624, p. 50). Cf. also Thomas Middleton's *Game at Chesse*, IV, i, 1–13.

vs without danger to exercise our Functions. Much more weighty is the salvation of our soules, then th'externall decency of our apparell; which though it be necessary in tyme and place; yet is it not soe essentiall a point, as for the Care therof to neglect the Charge of gods flock and the safety of our owne lives. *Dauid*[1] vpon iust cause feigned himself madd; but his madnes was an effect of perfect wisdome, and Reason the guide of his seeming folly. *Iudith*[2] laying aside her hayre-Cloth and widowes weede, disguised herself in such ornaments as were fitter to allure lascivious eyes, then to beare witnes of her sober mynde. And if god added grace 10 and beauty to her youthly dresses, to further her iust Revenge vpon her enemies: much more may we hope he will allow a lesse disguising in vs to reviue the soules of our dearest frends. It is noe sure Argument of inward vanity to be vaine in shew, sith a modest and an humble mynd may be shrowded vnder the glorious and Courtly Robes of a vertuous *Hester*.[3] And if Angells for the benefitt of bodies, haue suted their shapes to the request of their Ministeries, now appearing like soldiers, as to *Iosua*;[4] now like travellers, as to *Thobie*;[5] now like gratious youths, as to *Lott*;[6] yea, if *Christ*[7] himself as th'occasion required, seemed to the two disciples a Pilgryme, and 20 to *Saint Mary Magdalen* a Gardiner: why may not we for the wynning of soules (which (as god is our witnes) is th'only Cause of our Comming) frame our behavior and attyre to the necessity of our daies, as we we reade the auntient Bushops did in the persecution of the *Vandalls*.[8] This therfore cannot be esteemed a iust presumption of a *dissolute* mynd in vs, whom not any will to such finenes, but a desire of safety enforceth to weare the liveryes of the tyme.

4. Now wheras this heavy aduersary of our good names hath abused your Maiesties eares with a truthlesse surmise, *that we should avoide the Realme for lack of living*, we humbly resigne his folly to 30 the correction of your Highnes wisdome. For to whom can it seeme probable *that we flie for lack of living*, of whom many haue vowed, all willingly accepted a voluntary pouerty, leaving that we had, without either hope or Care of getting more; our wealth being now in well doing, and our patience our best possession. Is

[1] *Dauid*. See I Samuel xxi. 10–15.   [2] *Iudith*. See Judith x. 1–4.

[3] *Hester*, i.e. Esther.   [4] *Iosua*. See Joshua v. 13–15.

[5] *Thobie*. See Tobit v. 3–16.   [6] *Lott*. See Genesis xix. 1–3.

[7] *Christ*. See Luke xxiv. 18–35 and John xx. 11–18.

[8] *the persecution of the Vandalls*. In North Africa, A.D. 429–523.

it like that *for lack of living*, any would enter into a Course, wherin, without possibility of preferment they were in apparent hazard to loose their lives? Are any fled for such pouerty, that they could not at the least haue lived in service with more ease and lesse labour then they tie themselues vnto in a most streight life; wher they doe more by a willing obedience, then they should haue bene put to in a hired subiection? Or are they of such quality, and of so many pleasing parts, that they can in these severe tymes, winne men, with perill of their lands, lives and posterities to entertaine and
10 comfort them: and could they not haue found (without plunging themselues in a Sea of dangers) some more easy meanes for a Competent mayntenance, then to begg it out of so many Exigents, and wring it through soe grievous oppressions? And why should this feare of want pinch them more then infinite others whom they leave behinde them? They are men of as pregnant witts, as deliuer[1] tongues, as mature Iudgments, as most of the Inns of Court or Vniuersities where they lived. Yea they were already soe farr stept into promotion, that they needed to haue doubted nothing lesse then lack of living, diuers of them having bene Procters in vniuer-
20 sities, fellowes and officers of Colleges, and likely to haue risen to any higher preheminence, to omitt those that had Revenues and Annuyties of their owne, besides their Alliance and kindred with ritch and most wealthy families.

5. It pleaseth further this vnfreindly Informer (who seemeth best pleased with displeasing vs) to derive our departure from *a Conscience guilty of Crimes committed*, being still himself in the likenes of his speeches, as voyd of verity as full of ill will. For if Priests at their Arraignements be in a manner charged with Originall sinne, many of them haveing bene scarcely borne at the rising in
30 the North,[2] which is alwaies a Common place to declayme against them: If all the notorious faults that may any way concerne Catholiques are made ordinary inditements to condemne those that neuer heard of them, till they came to the barr: How much more would any fault of their owne be obiected, yea and multiplied in the vrgeing, if any such could haue bene found? But none yet was euer touched for any thing committed before his departure, as all testimonies may depose, and the very Records testifie in our behalfe.

[1] *deliuer*, agile.
[2] *the rising in the North.* The rising of the Catholic gentry in northern England in 1569 in favour of Mary, Queen of Scots.

And now to prevent any iust ground of this obloquy, the Superiours (not ignorant how many eyes are busied in watching for the least advantage against vs) make diligent scruteny for the perfect notice of their vertue, whom they admitt to Priesthood, who being for the most parte among many of their owne houses or standing in the Vniuersities, could not cloake any great enormity from notice: yea the very age of the greater parte (they going ouer very yonge)[1] is a warrant to acquitt them from any such offence as should force them to flie their Cuntrie; and others of riper yeares haue bene soe notefied for their morall life, that they haue made common report 10 their harbinger, to take vp their due rowmes in euery mans good opinion. In summe; this being an vnproved accusation, deliuered by one, that in the same discourse hath impanelled an Inquest of vntruthes, to finde him in this also guilty of falshoode, it needeth noe other answere but a wise Censure of the Reader.

6. But now (most mercifull Princesse) license our too-much wronged Innocency to rebate the sharpest dint of this vnkinde aduersary, pointed with these three odious termes of *Fugitiues*, *Rebells*, and *Traytors*; and dipped as deepe in the bitternes of his gaule, as he would haue it enter into our dearest bloud. And first 20 we Crave most humblye, but the right of Christians, beliefe of our Oath, which is the only Certificat to make our thoughts vndoubted: vpon hope wherof we oppose our guiltles hearts against these titles, as our best Armour of proofe; protesting vpon our soules and salvations, and calling Allmighty god and his Angells for witnesses, that as we hope to haue any benefitt by the most pretious wounds and death of our Lord *Jesus Christ*, the whole and only intent of our coming into this Realme, is noe other, but to labour for the salvation of soules, and in peaceable and quiet sort to confirme them in the auntient Catholique Faith in which their Fore- 30 fathers liued and died these 1400. yeares, and out of which we vndoubtedly belieue it is impossible that any soule should be saved. This from the sincerest of our thoughts before the throne of god we most truly professe, intending (if noe other remedy may be had) to let your Maiestie seale it with the best bloud that our faithfull and faultles hearts can afforde. And if any be soe hardened in a sett incredulity, as rather to condemne vs of periury, then to cleare vs vpon soe deepe an Oath, we will make Reason his guide into our

[1] *they going ouer very yonge.* Southwell himself went to Douay at the age of fourteen.

intentions, by which if he thinke vs not as much perished in our witts as he supposeth vs to be in our fidelity, he shall easily see the truth of our protestations. For first, *Treason* being an offence that carrieth with it such a stayne of Infamy as can neuer be taken out, and making those that committ it dead and vnpardonable persons: who can imagine any soe foolishlie desperate as to incurr soe reproachfull a Crime, full of certaine perills, having noe other possible marke for his hope, but the vttermost of all worldly evills. And if any one should chaunce to be soe farr distracted from his
10 sences, as to throw himself into soe bottomles a destruction; yet that so many soe learned and soe graue men as daily suffer for their comming in Priests,[1] would cast away their labours, lives, and Creditts, for nothing but a Cruell death, and an eternall reproach, our bitterest enemies could neuer deeme it likelie. And what other enticement should allure vs to be *Traytors*? not any perswasion that we our selues can Compasse soe great an exploit (there being scarce 300. Catholique Priests of our Nation in the whole world, a silly Army to subdue soe great a Monarchie): Not any Confidence in Catholiques assistance, whom none is soe madd to thinke able to
20 accomplish such an enterprise, being few in nomber, dispurveyed of munition, narrowly watched by Officers, restrained in their liberties, impoverished in their goods, and disabled in all provisions: Not the Imagination to be advanced by forreigne power; for then we would rather expect the Conquest, till the time and opportunity were ripe for vs to enter vpon our hopes, then soe venterouslie to presse vpon the swords of our enemies, and hazard not only our future expectations, but our present safeties: We would rather live abroad, though it were with as hard shifts, as those that now possesse honorable roumes did once at *Geneua*, then ieoperd
30 our wellfare to soe many, soe knowne, and soe inevitable harmes, which we are more likely soone to feele then soe long to eschue. And if we were to come as *Rebells* into the Realme, our education in Colleges should be answerable to that quality; we should be trayned in Martiall exercises, busied in pollitique and Civill affaires, hardened to the field, and made to the weapon; wheras a thousand eyes and eares are daily witnesses, that our studies are nothing ells but Philosophie and Devinity; our Teachers, Religious men,

---

[1] *for their comming in Priests.* By the statute 27 Eliz. c. 2 (1585) it was made treason for any priest ordained since the beginning of Elizabeth's reign to enter or remain in the kingdom.

acquainted with noe other knowledg but learning and vertue; all
our warlike preparations the wrastling with our wills, the morte-
fying of our bodies, and a continuall warrfare with nature, to get the
victory over our selues. And as for other *Schoole-points of Sedition*,
wherin this our hard Friend feigneth vs to be instructed, Allmighty
god is our witnes, that we neither learne nor teach any,[1] having
only had in our studies the common end that all men shoote at:
namely, to obtaine such knowledg as might be an ornament to our
function, a help to our Conuersation, and a benefit to our Cuntry.
But if by these *Schoole-points of Sedition* be meant that Religion   10
which there we are taught, and here we professe, this meaning
answereth it self. For this cannot any way be *treasonable* to your
Maiesties estate, vnless that be esteemed offensive which was the
Faith of all your royall Auncestors this 14. hundreth yeares, is the
Faith of the greatest parte of Christendome; and for the defence
wherof your Maiesties most worthy Father attayned the glorious
title of *Defendor of the Faith*. But whatsoeuer this Informer meant
by his *Schoole-points of Sedition*, we hope that your Highnes Censure
will free vs from the thing it self, syth neither likelyhood to effectuate any hope at home, nor any likenes[2] of our education abroad,   20
can in your wisdome seeme to argue vs guilty of any *Rebellious*
intentions. Let this further be an assured proofe to the Contrary,
that syth we are soe religiouslie addicted to the end of our Comming, that for the atcheiving therof we reckon our torments
triumphes, and our deaths a glory, if this end were the ouerthrow
of your Maiestie, or if your displacing had bene the point, that with
soe many bleeding wounds we haue witnessed to be soe deare vnto
vs, we could with the losse of fewer lives haue perfected our purpose, and long ere this haue brought the Cards to an vnfortunate
shuffling. For whosoeuer hath contemned his owne, is Master of   30
anothers life, and he that is resolute to spend his bloud, will rather
seeke to sell it for the intended prize, then with a fruitlesse effusion
Cast it away for noething.

Noe, noe, (most gratious Soueraigne) heauen and earth shall
witnes with vs in the dreadfull day of doome that our brests never

---

[1] *we neither learne nor teach any.* Allen was head of the seminary of Douay
for many years and, according to the *D.N.B.* article on him, 'it is a very
remarkable fact that he kept the work of the seminaries unmingled with his
political life'.

[2] *likenes.* Outward appearance, semblance.

harboured such horrible *Treasons,* and that the end of our Comming is the salvation of soules, not the murthering of bodies; we being rather willing to die then to contribute the least hayre of our heads to the later, and not soe willing to live as to shedd the best bloud of our bodies for the first. Give then (most excellent Queene) wise men leave to see, that they shew themselves noe lesse disloyall to your Maiestie, then iniurious to vs, that durst devulge these fables vnder the name of your Highnes, making their Prince the Patronesse of these feigned and devised falsehoods.

10   7. Now with what shadow of likelihoode can it sinke into any sound beliefe, that we come with ample authority to *perswade your Maiesties Subiects to renounce their duties, or to binde them with Oathes and Sacraments to forsweare their naturall Allegiance to your Highnes, or to yeald all their power or assistance to the Spanish forces.* For to say we doe it vpon hope to be enritched with those possessions that others now enioy hath but very small semblance of probability, considering how much likelyer we are to Inherit your Racks and possesse your places of Execution, then to surviue the present Incumbents of spirituall livings, or live to see any dignities at the
20 King of Spaines disposition. And sith both the daily Martyrdomes of many before our eyes and our owne evident and howerly dangers, cannot but kill in vs all such aspiring fancies, (if any mynd were soe muddy to sell his soule at soe base a rate) let it be scanned with Equity, how little seeming of truth it carrieth, that soe many should vpon soe vnprobable and vncertaine expectations expose their lives to most probable, and most certaine shipwracks. And can any imagine vs to be soe simple, that we cannot see how impossible it is for any Catholiques to doe the King any good, though they were as much bent that way as their Accusers would haue it thought?
30 Doe we not see that they are scattered one among thousands, and att all such occurrences soe well watched and soe ill provided, that to wish them to stirr in the Kings behalfe, were to trayne them to their vndoing, and to expose them to a generall massacre by domesticall fury? And what better Advocate can pleade for vs in this Cause, then your Maiesties owne experience, who in the last attempt of the King, found none more forward to doe all duties, or liberall to stretch their habilities, then Catholiques were in your Highnes defence. And allthough they were cessed[1] for men and money farr aboue their Revenues, and soe fleeced of their Armor and weapons,

----

[1] *cessed.* Assessed.

14

that they were left vnfurnished for their owne safeguard: yet were
they soe farr from mutening or touch of disloyaltie, that they
willingly yealded more then any other of their quality;. which
doubtles if Priests had sworne them with Oathes, or bound them
with Sacraments to the Contrary, they would neuer haue done, sith
they venture both lives and liberties for other Charitable workes of
farr lesse weight then th'avoyding of the damnable synnes of Periury
and Sacriledge. It is also well knowen, even to the Coyners of these
vntrue surmises, that if the King should come soe slenderly provided,
as to neede the handfull of Catholiques help, (who neither haue   10
Countenance Charge nor authority in the Common wealth) your
Maiestie neede not greatly feare him, sith it were impossible he
should be strong, to whom soe weake and booteles a succour should
be necessary. And to what effect should we then perswade Catholiques to leave their obedience to your Highnes sith it can neither
benefit vs nor availe them, but rather draw vpon vs both a manifest
subversion: yea did we not rather strengthen them in their duties,
and Confirme them in patience, and but that with Conscience and
religious feare they restrained nature, it were impossible for flesh
and bloud to disgest the vnmercifull vsage that they suffer by such   20
persons whose basenes doubleth the Iniury of their abuse. For who
(if it were not more then the feare of man that withhelld them)
would not rather die vpon their enemies that sought their bloud
(as for men soe ill mynded it were noe hard matter) then live only
to continuall deaths, and to leave the authors of their evills behinde
them to triumphe ouer their ruynes, and to send after them more
of their dearest Frends? What gentleman could endure the per-
emptory and insolent imperiousnes of a Company of greedy and
mannerles mates,[1] which are still praying vpon Catholiques as if
they were Common booties, and ransack them day and night,   30
braving them vnder their owne roofes with such surlynes, as if
euery Castaway were allowed to be vnto them an absolute Prince.

1. But happily because we desire to recouer the lapsed, and to
confirme the standing in the auntient Faith of their forefathers, it
may be presumed that this is a withdrawing from your Maiesties
obedience. But if Indifferency may be one of the Iury, disloyalty

---

[1] *mates.* To illustrate the contemptuous use of this word, the *O.E.D.*
quotes 'These witches are but lieng mates and couseners' (Reginald Scot's
Discoverie of Witchcraft), and 'These Iesuits are cogging mates' (T. James's
The Jesuits Downefall, 1612).

shall never be found the sequell of any Article of our Religion; which more then any other tieth vs to a most exact submission to your temporall authority, and to all points of Allegiance, that either now in Catholique Cuntries, or euer before in Catholique tymes, were acknowledged to be due to any Christian Prince. Doe not now Catholiques governed by the principles of their Faith, yeald, in respect therof, with a knowen mildnes, their goods, liberties, lands, and lives? And doe they not with a most resolute patience obey a scourging and afflicting hand? Then how much more would
10 they be willing to double their duties and increase their serviceable affections to your Highnes, if they found but the like Clemency that other subiects enioy and were not made (as now they are) Common steeles for every mercilesse and flint-harted man to strike out vpon them the sparkles of his fury. It is a point of the Catholique Faith (defended by vs against the Sectaries of these dayes) that Subiects are bound in Conscience, vnder paine of forfeiting their right in heaven, and incurring the guilt of eternall torments, to obey the iust Lawes of their Princes; which both the Protestants and Puritans deny with their Father *Mr Calvin*. And therefore if we
20 were not pressed to that which by the generall verdict of all ages was iudged a breach of the Law of god, we should neuer give your Maiestie the least Cause of displeasure. For, excepting those points, which (if impartiall audience were allowed) we could prove to implie the endles misery and damnation of our soules, in all other Civill and temporall respects, we are as submitted and pliable as any of your Maiesties best beloved subiects. If then your Highnes would vouchsafe to behould our Case with an vnveyled eye, and not view vs in the mirror of a misinformed mynde, we would not doubt, but that your excellent wisdome would finde more grounds,
30 even in pollicy, and in the due Care of your owne safety to encline your gratious favour towards vs, then to keep vs still enthralled in our present vnhappines.

2. But it may be that some, more willing to ripp vp old faults, then to admitt any clearing of them when in their hearts they haue already condemned vs to all punishments, will here bring in *Ballards* and *Babingtons* matters against vs, as a *Golias*[1] to ouerthrow all other proofes of our good meanings. To this first we answere, that it were a hard Course to reproue all Prophetts for one *Saul*,[2] all Protestants

[1] *Golias.* See I Samuel xvii. 4–11.
[2] *Saul.* See I Samuel x. 1–13.

for one *Wyatt*,[1] all Priests and Catholiks for one *Ballard* and *Babing-ton*. Your Maiesties Sister reigned not the sixt parte of your time, and yet nyne sundry Rebellions were attempted by the Protestant faction against her in that short space, as euery Chronicle can witnes, wheras in this your Maiesties prosperous Raigne of 33. yeares in all England the Catholiques neuer rose but once[2] in open field to haue wonne the freedome of their Consciences, which the Protestants, in those five yeares laboured with so many mutenies. For as for *Parry*,[3] he neuer in life or action professed himself to be a Catho-lique: yea and he took it offensiuely, with signification of his mynd 10 in hott words, that some vpon surmise had soe named him. And therfore howsoever he might by aspiring thoughts or mercinary motives be by any forreigne enemy vsed to ill practises, it cannot iustly be layd against vs, whom neither privity nor consent to his Intentions can any way touch.

And as for this Action of *Babington*, it was in truth rather a snare to entrap them, then any devise of their owne, sith it was both plotted, furthered and finished by Sir *Francis Walsingham* and his other Complices, who layd and hatched all the particulers therof, as

---

[1] *Wyatt*. Sir Thomas Wyatt's rebellion early in Mary's reign (1554) was on behalf of Elizabeth, and was the immediate cause of the execution of Lady Jane Grey.

[2] *but once*. The Rising in the North, 1569.

[3] *Parry*. William Parry was a Welshman who, after dissipating his own and his wife's fortunes, stabbed one of his creditors almost to death. He was arrested, tried and sentenced to death, but received the Queen's pardon. Thereafter he went abroad and spent several years in the Low Countries and France. For a time he acted as a secret agent for Burleigh, sending him reports on the Catholics and their designs. He returned to England in 1584 and frankly admitted to the Queen herself that he had been in touch with the papal secretary and the agents of the Queen of Scots in Paris, and had even discussed with them projects for Elizabeth's assassination. He was a member of the 1584 Parliament, and created a sensation by speaking against the bill to make it treason for a priest or Jesuit to enter the kingdom. Soon after-wards, on his own initiative and apparently with the intention of incrimin-ating his victim, he broached another plot for assassinating the Queen to Edmund Neville, claimant to the barony of Latimer. But Neville betrayed Parry first, and, though Neville was sent to the Tower, Parry was executed for treason on 2 March 1585.

All the orthodox accounts of Parry and his treason speak of him as a violent Catholic, but, in view of what is now known of him and his activities, Southwell's statements about his religion may well be true. On Parry see further Conyers Read, *Mr Secretary Walsingham*, II, 399–405.

they thought it would best fall out to the discredit of Catholiques, and cutting off the *Queene* of *Scotts*. For first it is knowne to all, that *Poolie*[1] being Sir *Francis Walsinghams* man, and throughlie seasoned to his Masters tooth, was the chiefe Instrument to contrive and prosecute that matter, and to draw into the nett such greene witts, as (partly fearing the generall oppression, partly angled with golden hookes) might easily be ouerwrought by Master Secretaries subtill and sifting witt. For *Poolie* masking his secrett Intentions vnder the face of Religion, and abusing with irreligious hypocrasie 10 all Rites and Sacraments, to borrow the false opinion of a Catholique still fedd the poore gentlemen with his Masters baytes, and he holding the lyne in his hand, suffered them like silly fish to play themselues vpon the hooke, till it were throughly fastened, that then he might strike at his owne pleasure, and be sure to draw them to a Certaine destruction. And though none were soe deepe in the very bottome of that Conspiracy as *Pooly* himself, yet was he not so much as Indicted of any Cryme, but after a little large Imprisonment (more of Pollicy then any punishment) sett at liberty, and in more Credit then euer he was before. For this being a sett match, 20 and he having soe well performed his evill parte, though to please babes a stroke were given to beate him, yet doubtles he was largely fedd in his privy pay, as soe vnchristian a Pollicy did well deserue. It is alsoe knowne by *Philips* the Decipherers[2] letters to his partie practitioner *Gilbert Gifford*,[3] in whose Chest and Chamber they

---

[1] *Poolie.* The completest account of Robert Poley or Poolie is to be found in F. S. Boas's *Christopher Marlowe, a Biographical and Critical Study*, chapters 8, 16 and 17. Poley was an agent of Walsingham who managed to insinuate himself into the confidence of the adherents of Mary, Queen of Scots, and became particularly intimate with Babington and his friends. However, he was not, as Southwell states, directly in the service of Walsingham, but of Walsingham's daughter, Lady Sidney, wife of Sir Philip.

[2] *Philips the Decipherer.* Thomas Philips or Phelippes was a confidential secretary of Walsingham famous for his skill in deciphering documents written in code. All the intercepted correspondence of Mary, Queen of Scots passed through his hands, and he has been credited with the forgery of the postscript of Mary's fatal letter to Babington. See Conyers Read, *op. cit.* III, 37–46.

[3] *Gilbert Gifford.* Another of Walsingham's secret agents. A kinsman of William Gifford, one of the leaders of the secular faction and later Archbishop of Rheims, Gilbert Gifford belonged to an old Catholic family and was educated at Rome and Rheims. He returned to England in 1585, but was immediately arrested and taken to Walsingham. Thereafter he played a double

were taken at Paris, and by *Gilbert Giffords* owne examinations, that these gentlemen were bought and sould, being drawne blind-fould to be the workers of their owne overthrow, and to carry with seelie *Isaac*[1] the fier and fewell in which they themselues were to be sacrificed. And since, it is knowne that all the letters that fedd them with forreigne hopes, all the devises that wrought them into home-bred Imaginations, sprong all out of the same fountayne of Sir *Francis* his fine head. For *Gilbert Gifford* having some yeares before bene Master Secretaries Intelligencer (as the date of *Philips* letters vnto him discovered) when the matter was once on foote in 10 *England* was made the meane to follow it in *France* among certaine of the *Scottish Queenes* Frends, more apt to enter then able to goe through great designements, where he knowing of the letters, and the Course how they were conveyed,[2] discovered all to Master Secretary, to whom also he brought divers of like tenor, written partly to the *Queene* partly to *Babington* at his owne Comming into *England*: which was more then three moneths before the Counsaile would seeme to know these Intentions. And when by often resort to Sir *Francis Walsinghams* house in privie sort, he had taken of him further directions; to make his Course the more plausable for his 20 proceedings in *Fraunce*, he practised here with the French Ambassador *Monsieur Chatteneufe*, whom then he knew to be very well affected both to the *Queene* of *Scotts* and the *Duke* of *Guise*. And though he were accounted a man of more then ordinary discourse, yet with soe forsworne an hypocrasy and soe deepe periuries did *Gifford* ouer-reach him, that when the trayne was discouered, some of his gentlemen enraged with soe great impiety, sayd, that though it were a parte of the gospell that an Englishman would be true, they should hardlie belieue it for that divell *Giffords* sake, as in their passion they termed him. But soe it was, that *Gilbert Giffords* witt, 30 being farr to good for soe bad an owner, and newly refined in

part. He and Poley were Walsingham's principal means of contact with the agents of Mary and with Babington and his friends.

Gifford fled to France shortly before the arrest of the conspirators, and was ordained priest at Rheims. He was arrested in a Paris brothel in 1587, and died in prison in 1590. The papers seized after his arrest have not survived.

[1] *Isaac.* See Genesis xxii. 6–9.

[2] *knowing of the letters, and the Course how they were conveyed.* For a time Gifford acted as an intermediary through whom all the secret correspondence of Mary, Queen of Scots passed. Through his means the letters all came into the hands of Philips before being delivered to their destinations.

Master Secretaries forge, wonne so much Credit, that he being commended and believed, as his desire was, he went ouer to entreate by meanes with the *Duke* of *Guise*, and such others as were thought fitt to be taken in as stales, to countenance the matter, and to put the gentlemen in vaine expectations, till the thredd were spunne to the intended length. And soe farr was this infortunate wretch given ouer to desperate malice, that first, to possesse him more of Master Secretaries good opinion, and to shew his aptness to be vsed in such exploits, he dedicated to him a booke of his owne Compiling,[1] breathing such Infamies and Atheismes as best became the spirit of soe periured an Apostata. And on th'other side to shunne the suspition of being Master Secretaries bad Instrument in this vnchristian Pollicy, he was, as he himself Confessed, purposely graduated, and (as it is thought) made Priest: Soe impious were the meanes to wrest the poore gentlemen from their duties to their owne Confusion. *Phillips* alsoe, who was then Master Secretaries right hand, helld Correspondencye with *Gilbert Gifford*, still keeping the Ice from breaking, till all were vpon it whom they meant to drowne in the same destruction. And to drawe the *Queene* of *Scotts* into the better opinion of this designement (whom experience had taught to suspect such dangerous motions) the matter was with continuall and secrett meetings very seriouslie vrged with her Agents in France, in whom it is feared that she relied too much affiance: but whether for love to their Mistress they were too apt to entertaine any hope of her deliuery, or for league with Master Secretary too ready to build vpon his foundations, they induced the *Queene* to like of their good will, that were willing to adventure their estates and lives to doe her service. And as things by these Inventions were ripening in *Fraunce*; soe *Poolie* noe lesse diligently plyed his taske at home, continually conuersing with *Ballard*[2] and the gentlemen, and labouring to draw more Conyes into the hay: It is strange to marke with what Cunning the graver and wiser sort of Catholikes were sounded afarr of, not by revealing any direct intention, but soe nicely glauncing at generall points, with yfs and ands, that they neuer vnderstood the language, till effects did Conster those roving speeches: yet when so much of their disposition was

---

[1] *a booke of his owne Compiling.* This was a book, never published, written against the Jesuits. See *Mary Queen of Scots and the Babington Plot*, ed. J. H. Pollen (Scottish Historical Society), pp. cxix–xx and cciii.

[2] *Ballard.* John Ballard was the only priest among the conspirators.

knowne by their vnwillingnes to heare, and peremptorines in
Cutting of the offers of such discourses, there was noe lesse Care
vsed to Conceale these purposes from them, then there had bene
Covine[1] to search out how they would deeme of them: For it
was feared their wisdome would haue found out the fraude, and
vntimely haue launced an vnripe Impostume. It is further knowne,
that the Coppy of that letter which *Babington* sent to the *Queene*
of *Scotts*, was brought him ready penned by *Poolie* from Master
Secretary, the answere wherof was the principall ground of the
Queenes Condemnation. There was also found in Sir *Francis Walsing-*   10
hams accompts after his decease, a note of 7000 *li.* bestowed vpon
Naw and *Curle*,[2] who being the *Queenes* Secretaries, framed such
an answere as best might serue for the ditty of a bloudy Ryme, and
fitt his intention that rewarded them with soe liberall a Fee. This
made *Phillips* soe bould to advise *Gifford* by his letters, that if he
came in any suspition of detecting the *Queene* he should lay it either
vpon *Nawe* or *Curle*, whose shoulders being boulstred with soe
large bagges, he thought would be best able to beare the burthen
away. It is also certaine, that *Bernard Mawde*[3] (Master Secretaries
vndoubted Agent) went ouer into Fraunce with *Ballard*, about this   20
practise, their free passage being warranted with all security; and
when they had bene there soe long that *Bernard* might looke into
their proceedings who in those Cuntries were actors in the matter,
he returned againe with *Ballard*, and having a large Commission
from Sir *Francis Walsingham* to take what nomber of horses he
would out of any gentlemans Parke or Pasture, and of other vnvsuall
liberties, he went with *Ballard* into the North; there he sought by
what slights he could to haue wound in divers gentlemen, making
Ballards credit his Countenance, and drawing the poore man to be
vnwittingly the occasion of his owne and others ruyne. In th'end   30
having Cosened another to gett a letter of Commendations to the
Lord Prior of Scotland, he sifted out of him what he could, and
taking with him a letter touching this matter, he brought it with

[1] *Covine*. Fraud, treachery.

[2] *Naw and Curle*. Claude Nau de la Boisselière and Gilbert Curll, Queen
Mary's two secretaries. Both were forced to give evidence against her at her trial.

[3] *Bernard Mawde*. Another of Walsingham's agents. He was sentenced to
imprisonment in 1583 for having blackmailed the Archbishop of York, but
was released, apparently at Walsingham's intercession and on condition that
he became a spy. He seems to have been assigned the task of keeping watch
on Ballard.

all the Intelligence and successe of his malitious Pilgrymage, to the Counsell. And though he were thus inward and conversant with *Ballard*, carrying him to sundry gentlemen of account, to feele and tempt them about this action, and to draw them into the desired Compasse: yea though himself were a motioner to some to enter into it, pretending that he had ouer-reached Master Secretary in getting that Commission; yet was he neuer called to the barr, but hyred to stay a tyme in restraint, with such a recompence for his service as might well be perceaved to be large, by his liberall spending 10 and plenty in prison, he being otherwise a hungry and needy merchant, without either trade or living to mayntaine such expences.

And how privy Sir *Francis* was to the whole Course of the gentlemens Actions, and to the certaine period of tyme wherin all his endeavours would come to the full point, may be gathered by this; that being by a Priest that was to be banished[1] sued vnto for 20. daies respitt to dispatch his busines, first repeating the nomber, and pausing a while with himself: Noe sayth he, you shall haue but 14: for if I should graunt you any more, it would be to your hinderance, as you shall heare hereafter. Wherin he sayd true: for 20 much about that tyme was publike notice taken of *Babingtons* matter, all high wayes were watched, infinite houses searched, hues and Cries raised, frights bruted in the peoples eares, and all mens eyes filled with such a smoake, as though the whole Realme had bene on fier, wheras in truth it was but the hissinge of a few greene twigges of their owne kindling, which they might without any such vprores haue quenched with a handfull of water, but that it made not so much for their purpose as these buggish and terrible shewes. And though they were soe well acquainted with all the gentlemens haunts, that they might every hower in the day or 30 night haue drawne them into the nett like a Covy of Partridges: yet forsooth must some of them be purposely suffered to flie, that they might haue the better Colour to make those generall demonstrations of a needles feare. *Iohn Savage*[2] likewise when he came vnto

---

[1] *a Priest that was to be banished.* According to Pollen (*op. cit.* p. cli) this priest was Martin Aray, who was banished about this time.

[2] *Iohn Savage.* Savage had been educated at Douay and had served in the Spanish armies in the Low Countries. He confessed that he had taken a vow to assassinate Elizabeth. He came to England in the latter half of 1585 and, probably through the influence of Gifford, with whom he had been intimate on the Continent, was induced to join forces with Babington. He was captured and executed with the other conspirators.

the Court, was soe well knowne to be a Chicken of that fether, that two Pensioners were charged to haue a spetiall eye vpon him, and to watch him soe long as he stayed there, and yet was he suffered to goe vp and downe the Court, and vsually to haunt the Presence, till all the Irons were hott that were layd in the fier to seere the Creditt of poore Catholiques and to giue the *Queene* of *Scotts* her deaths wound. It is also noted, that after *Ballard* was enchaunted with *Poolies* charmes, he became a stranger to all the Iesuites and other Priests, being limited, by the pollitique Rules of his Prompter, to such Company as Master Secretary knew to be of 10 dimme sight to see through so many mists as he by his Instruments had already cast before their eyes. The gentlemen also were throughlie Charmed to keepe their Counsells from the wiser and maturer sort of Catholiques when there was noe hope to make them parties: of which, though *Iohn Charnock*[1] at the barr sayd the reason to be because the oulder the Coulder; yet the true ground was a spetiall Proviso of Master Secretary, to keep the thredd out of their hands that would soone haue vnwound it to the bottome. For what man that had but knowne the first sillables of Pollicy, could thinke it a likely course from them to alter the whole State of soe 20 great a Monarchie to quite contrary Religion and gouernment, that neither had forreyne power to back them (as then there was none ready) nor helpes at home to support them, being all but private gentlemen, neither of wealth nor sufficient Credit to carry with them any great nombers. Yea who would not haue pittied their indiscretion, that intending soe great an alteration, thought it a fitt way to goe picking vp here and there one, as if such plotts, in so many yonge tongues, could lie hidden soe long, as to giue them respite to gleane a sufficient Army. And for men that pledged their heads in soe dangerous attempts, to be soe credulous as to rest their 30 hopes vpon flying Reports and faire promises of forreyne helpes, without the certainty of such preparations of shipps and men as might come in due tyme to follow their beginnings, was a most Childish ouersight. And therfore to any man of experience that had looked into it, there would haue offered it self a iust suspition, that the plott was rather a trayne to entrap the actors in it, then a meane to effect that which was intended by it. For though they had cutt of some of the Counsell, yea and dismantled the Realme

---

[1] *Iohn Charnock.* Another of the conspirators; a friend of Savage, with whom he had served in the Low Countries.

of her sacred Maiestie (which gods goodnes neither would, nor we hope will permitt) yet had their purpose bene farr from any semblance of their desired Issue. For then they must either haue proclaymed the *Queene* of *Scotts*, or at the least by some meanes haue sought her delivery, and consequently haue notefied to the world, that for her rising was your Maiesties going downe, and what a tide of resistance this notice would haue brought in, none can be soe seelie but he must needs see. For first by the Oath of Association,[1] all the Nobility had byn bound to pursue her to death,

10 which many without an Oath would otherwise haue bene apt enough to doe. The Crowne also being left without any declared owner, as a faire goale for them that could first come at it, noe doubt but diuers Competitors would haue hindered her Course, to haue made their hopes way to soe faire an ayme. Then th'Act of Parliament[2] excluding strangers from the Crowne (as she by diuers meanes was devulged to be) would also haue added danger to her Clayme, espetially considering th'auntient and deepe rooted dislike betwene the Scottish and the English, noe small motiue to a populer muteny. But most of all her vehemency in the Catholique Religion

20 (against which, both the Nobility Clergy and Commons were most violently bent) would haue made them ready in that respect to take holld of the least of these letts to exclude her from the Crowne, and to translate the title to some other more suteable to their beliefe. All which Impediments meeting so full with euery eye, that did but look towards them, must needs haue made any in reason to conclude it an impossibility for those gentlemen to haue compassed their drift; which they also might easily haue discerned, had they not bene bewitched with Master Secretaryes fine devices, and deluded with his Spies Cosening letters and messages from forreigne

30 parts. For the Spanish fleete was not ready in two yeares after: and in *France* (more then a few that in *Gascoigne* were imployed against the *Hugenotts*) there was noe kinde of provision by sea or land. Yea the King was even then knowne to be so sure a friend to *England* and soe sharp an enemy to the *Guisian* partie (in which the

---

[1] *Oath of Association.* After the assassination of the Prince of Orange in 1584 groups of Englishmen bound themselves together to defend the Queen from a similar fate. They vowed that, if she should be killed, they would put to death the person for whose sake she had been murdered, viz. Mary, Queen of Scots.

[2] *the Act of Parliament.* The Act of Succession, 1534.

Queenes affiance was only fastened) that he would never haue suffered her hopes to haue had effect by any French assistance. And from *Scotland* they neuer looked for any ayde knowing (if they were not euery way blinde) how the King was wholly carried away with an English byas, and soe setled in the possession of his Crowne, and the bent of a Contrary Faith, that whatsoeuer he might haue attempted for himself, it was neuer likely he would haue followed their designment, of which the principall scope was th'alteration of Religion. And he that in respect of his beliefe, refused with the Infanta of Spaine the present possession of the low Cuntries, assistance for the Challenge of his other titles, and a promise to be proclaymed heire, if the Spanish Prince should faile, was doubtles much better armed against their slender perswasions, which could neuer haue tempted him with soe glorious offers. Finally the weaknes of this beginning was an apparent profe, that it was conceaved and bred by them, that would be sure to bring it to an abortion, and neuer suffer it to prevaile to any other purpose, but to make vs more hatefull, and to bereave your Maiestie of your more infamed then faultie Cousin.

Thus (most gratious Soueraigne) is your Highnes drawne, by these indirect Courses, to vse your vnwilling sword, against your lesse favoured then faithfull subiects, and put in vngrounded feares of their disloyalty, who are, of them selues, soe farr from defiling their hearts with any treasonable thoughts, that their heaviest enemies had no other meanes to dismount them from their best deserving, but by violenting[1] them to evill by these sinister inventions. We know your Maiesties mynd to be free from yealding your royall assent to soe ougly shifts, you euer bounding your desires to the limitts of vertue, and measuring your Regality more by will to saue then by power to kill. Yet it cannot but afflict vs to see your Highnes eares soe guarded against our Complaints, and possessed with their perswasions that most maligne vs, that we can haue noe other Orators for your gratious favour, then their tongues which cannot afford vs any favourable word. It hath byn alwaies the Pollicy of our Aduersaries, to keep vs aloofe from revealing our vniust oppressions, least they should enclyne your Maiesties mercy to pitty vs: And they fore-arme your Highnes with soe hard Informations against vs, that they make our very sute for lenity seeme an offensive motion. Yet sith we must either speake or die,

[1] *violenting*. Constraining.

seeing soe many slights are put in ure[1] to bury vs quick in all miseries, we hope god will make our Petitions way vnto your Maiesties heart, and winne your Clemency to consider our distresse, notwithstanding the slaunders that are published against vs. And if we may make our benefitt of that which others haue vsed to our greatest harmes, we thinke that this very Action of *Babingtons*, may assure your Highnes of the impossibility of Catholiques to be drawne to Rebellion. For when our oppressions were heaviest, our deaths ordinary, and soe fine witts busied in trayning vs into the
10 toyle; yet was there not in all England, in soe long tyme, found aboue one Priest,[2] and he one of the meanest, and few more then a dozen lay men that could be found to stoupe to these odious lures. Let not therfore this more preiudice vs, then soe open threats and direct menacings to the whole State haue endomaged others; sith of our side there followed noe effects, and our nombers were lesse likely to hurt, not ariving to a score, then theirs which dared your Maiesties scepter with many thowsands. But because we, like god Almightyes fooles (as some scornefully call vs) lay our shoulders vnder every loade, and are contented to make Patience our only
20 salve for all soares, many that see, are willing to vse the awe of our Consciences for their warrant to tread vs downe, wheras they presume not to meddle with others, though more fatall to your Highnes estate, knowing that if they should make them but partners of half our afflictions, they would soone bewray more impatient stomakes. For if the working of their spiritts be soe vehement, as with soe little feare, and with so much solempnity to proclayme a new *Christ*[3] and King of the earth, adding the Crest of an vsurped Messias to Countenance the Challenge of humane Soveraignty; If being soe freely permitted to vse their Consciences to themselues,
30 and to enioy their honours, offices, and favours in the Common wealth, without any taste of scourges; they notwithstanding sparkle out such tokens of a Concealed flame; It cannot but be seene and knowne how much more Cause there is to looke into their actions, and to feare their attempts, then to wreake such anger vpon vs,

---

[1] *ure.* Use, effect. [2] *one Priest.* Viz. John Ballard.

[3] *proclayme a new Christ.* A reference to the crazy Puritan fanatic, William Hacket, who on 19 July 1591 proclaimed himself Messiah from a cart in Cheapside. He called on the people to repent and follow him, claiming spiritual and civil jurisdiction superior to that of the Queen. He was immediately arrested and charged with treason. He suffered a traitor's death a few days later.

that were neuer Chargable with soe huge enormities. And yet the death of one man shut vp in a silent oblivion that open offer to an vprore, and most blasphemous Impiety against god and your Maiestie, though it be generally knowne that there were more favourers and Abettors of that party then could euer be touched with *Babingtons* offence.

We speake not this to incense your Maiestie against others, being too well acquainted with the smart of our owne punishments to wish any Christians to be partakers of our paines. Our only intent is, most humbly to intreate, that if soe impatient a zeale, accom- 10 panied with soe seditious words and actions, was soe easily finished and remitted in the Chastisement of one, your Highnes in Clemency would not suffer so many innocent Priests and Catholiques to be soe cruelly and continually martyred, who neuer incurred soe enor- mous Crymes. And sith we daily in our lives, and allwayes at our executions, vnfeynedly pray for your Maiestie: sithence at our deaths we all protest vpon our soules, our Clearnes from Treason, and our loyall and dutifull mynds, subscribing our protestations with our dearest bloud: Let us not (most mercifull Soueraigne) be thus daily plunged deeper into new disgraces, and still proclaymed 20 and murthered for Traytors. Let vs not be esteemed soe godles and desperate Monsters, as to spend our last breath in booteles periuries, or at our greatest neede of gods favour to sacrifice to the Divell our finall vowes. What reason can there move vs soe damnably to dissemble, when our expired date cutteth of all hopes? our death, the end of evills, hath in this world noe after feares; and a resolute Contempt of our owne lives excludeth all thoughts of meaner loves. Yea if any hope, feare, or love carry then any sway (as doubtles there doth in all Christian mynds) it is a hope to be saved, a feare to be damned, a love to god, to his truth, and to our endles well 30 being: All which, in that dreadfull moment (whervpon dependeth a whole eternity) can neuer be motives vnto vs to send our forsworne soules headlong to hell fier.

8. But let vs proceede in our necessary defence, as the Inditor doth in his false accusations. We are charged (for the easier attrac- tion of vnnaturall people and weake of vnderstanding to yeald to our perswasions) *to haue brought Bulls and Indulgences, pretending to promise heauen, or Cursings threatning damnation or hell.* It was but a barraine supply, for want of true faults to fasten vpon vs this fond Collusion, being soe farr from truth, and soe full of Incongruity, 40

27

that euery Novice in our Faith can reprove it of error. We remitt the reprochfull termes of *vnnaturall and weake of vnderstanding*, most iniuriously fathered vpon such a Princesse penn, whom a Royall mynd and Maiestie hath taught, not to staine her paper or blemish her stile with these and so many other base and reviling words as are pestered together in this Proclamation. We report all men to their eyes and eares for the answere of these slaunders, whether (their soule-rights excepted) in all temporall duties, Catholiques be not as *naturall* to their Prince, as beneficiall to their Neighbours, as reguler
10 in themselues as any other subiects, yealding the vttermost of all that is expected in Subsidies, Loanes, men and munition, besides the patient losse of their goods and lands for their Recusancy. Let it be read in letters of experience whether Catholiques be of soe shallow braine, or of soe weake vnderstanding, that they could be caried away with these imaginary *Bulls, promising heauen or threatning hell*, of which Catholiques eares neuer heard of before. This the world can witnes, that in Devinity, Law, Phisick, and all other faculties or functions either of piety or pollicy, all England, we may say all Christendome scarce knoweth any more renowned then our
20 English Catholiques (without vanity be it spoken in a iust defence). But though they were not such *Salomons* for wisdome as some others take themselues to be; yet they may be allowed ordinary sence and intendment, which if it be but so much as may serue them to tell ouer the Articles of their Creede, it is enough to know that noe *Bull* can otherwise *promise heauen or threaten hell*, but for keeping or breaking gods Commaundements. Iudg then (most Soueraigne Lady) whether it be not too great an indignity, to see the sacred name of our *Queene* (which next vnto gods word should be honoured among the most impregnable testimonies of truth) to be,
30 with vndeserued abuse, by any subiect subscribed to these impossible Fictions.

9. Who likewise (but meaning to make his Princes penn a spring of vntruthes) would against the certaine knowledg of infinite seers and hearers, deliuer, as from your Maiestie, that noe Priest is indited, arraigned, or executed for Religion, sith it is in euery Sessions seene, that vnles we ourselues should Confesse that we were Priests, noe other treasonable Cryme could be iustly proved against vs. And as for this, how farr it is from deseruing this odious title, your Maiestie may easily gather, for that all Christendome hath
40 these 1500. yeares honoured for Pastors and gouernours of their

28

soules, those that are now more then vnfavourably termed *Traytors*.
Yea, if to be a Priest made by th'authority of the Sea of *Rome*, and
present within your Highnes dominions, be a iust title of *Treason*:[1]
If they that relieue, harbour, or receave any such be worthy to be
deemed fellons; then all the glorious Saints of this land, (whose
vertue and doctrine god Confirmed with many Miracles) were noe
better then Traytors, and their Abettors Fellons: then *Damianus*
and *Fugatius*,[2] that first brought Christianity into our Cuntry in
King *Lucius* time, 1400. yeares past: then Saint *Augustine* and his
Company, that Converted our Realme in Saint *Gregories* time were 10
all within the Compasse of *Treason*, sith their Functions and ours
were all one, equally derived from the See of *Rome*, from whence
they were directly by the Popes, *Eleutherius*[3] and *Gregory* sent into
this Kingdome, being Priests and Religious men, as all antiquity
doth witnes; yea all the Churches and places of piety, chiefe
ornaments of this noble Realme, all the Charters and endowments
bestowed vpon Priests and Religious persons, and yet registred in
the auntient Lawes, are but Monuments of Felony and favourers of
treason. And if it should please god to allott the day of generall
Resurrection in your Maiesties tyme (a thing not soe impossible as 20
vncertaine) what would so many Millions of Prelates, Pastors, and
Religious people thinke, that both honoured and blessed this
Kingdome with the holiness of their life and excellency of their
learning? Much would they rest amazed to see their Reliques burned,
their Memories defaced, and all Monasteries, dedicated once to
Chastity, prayer, and piety, now either buried in their owne ruynes,
or profaned by vnfitting vses. But much more would they muse
to finde their Priesthood reckoned for Treason, and the reliefe of
Priests condemned for Felony, these being the two principall testimonies of devotion that their ages were acquainted with. Yea what 30
would your Maiesties predecessors and Fathers, with the Peeres and
people of your Realme thinke, when they should see themselues

[1] *if to be a Priest...be a iust title of Treason.* A reference to the Statute
of 1585.

[2] *Damianus and Fugatius.* The story of the conversion of King Lucius by
these two missionaries is one of Geoffrey of Monmouth's fables (*Historia Regum
Britanniae*, IV, xix). In Geoffrey their names are Duvianus and Faganus,
but by Elizabethan times their names had been corrupted to the forms
given here.

[3] *Eleutherius.* The Pope who was credited with having sent Damianus and
Fugatius to England.

in termes of Felony by the Censure of your Lawes, for erecting
Bushopricks, endowing Churches, founding Colleges, and such
other like places for the honouring and mayntayning Priests and
Religious men; yea and for giving their ghostly Fathers in way of
reliefe but a Cupp of colde water, though it were at the very point
of death, when they most needed spirituall Comforts, being then
to abandon their mortall bodies. And though the Priests of those
times were not made since the first yeare of your Highnes raigne,
which is the only point that exempteth them from the Statute: yet
10 were they all such Priests or Abettors of them, as were consecrated
by authority derived from the Sea of Rome, as all Registers doe
record, and present within your Maiesties Realme, which are the
only materiall points for which we haue bene or can be condemned.
For the Sea of Rome remayning in the self same Estate still, endued
with the same authority, and neither the manner of our Creation,
nor the Priesthood in it self in the least mynume altered from that it
was: why should it be more treasonable to be made Priest on the
Midsomer day of your first yeare, then the next day before, or the
last of *Queene Maries* Raigne. For neither doth the Pope, nor any
20 other Bushop, by making vs Priests, clayme or gett any more
authority in our Realme, then they of *Basill* or *Geneua* by making
Protestant Ministers; nor we by receaving our Orders from him,
acknowledg in him any mites worth of authority more then every
Lay Catholique doth throughout Christendome. And as for Oathes
and promises in receaving holy Orders, we neither take nor plight
any, but one Common to the Priests of all Nations, which is
a solemne Vowe of perpetuall Chastity, a thing rather pleasing then
offensive to a vertuous *Queene*, who hath for her self made Choise
of a single life. And who then can finde any colourable pretence to
30 verifie this slaunder, more grievous vnto vs then death it self, *that
we are not condemned and executed for Religion, but for Treason*, we
being allwayes arraigned and Cast vpon the Statute of Coming
into England, being since the first of your Maiesties Raigne made
Priests by authority of the See of Rome. For what can be meant by
Religion if it be not a point, yea and a Chiefe point therof, to receave
a Sacrament of the Catholique Church, (as we acknowledg Priesthood to be) of the chiefe pastor and prelate therof, from whence we
can proue all lawfull Priesthood to haue descended these 1500.
yeares? And to avouch vs *Traytors* for coming into England or
40 remayning here, is an Iniury without ground, sith in this respect

30

the Statute could not touch vs, setting Priesthood aside, many comming in and going out at their pleasure without any such sup-posall of *Treason*. But it is our Comming in as Priests that is soe highlie condemned, and therfore our Priesthood and nothing ells is punished by this Lawe. And howbeit the Chiefe devisers of this and all like decrees (euer seeking to attire their drifts against Religion vnder some other pretence) exempted the *Queene Mary* Priests from the Compasse of this Statute by a limitation of tyme; yet was that but a colour to inveigle such eyes, as either through Carelessnes would not looke, or through weakenes could not reach 10 into their finall intentions: And little regarded they a few very olde and feeble men, whom either age by course of nature, or they by other Arts might soone cutt of, soe the seede might be extinguished, and a new supply of posterity prevented, which by this lawe (though in vaine) they purposed to doe. Be it therfore neuer so much mistitled with the vndeserved name of *Treason*, the basenes of the reproach cannot cover the truth from your Maiesties best discerning insight, which by this cannot but apparentlie see, that it is, it was, and euer wilbe Religion, and nothing but Religion, for which we expose our bloud to the hazard of these Lawes, and for 20 the benefit of soules yeald our bodies to all extremities. It may be also easily gathered, by the weakest witts, what huge *Treasons* they be, for which we are condemned, sith at our Arraignments and deaths we are offered that once going to the Church should wipe away the heynousnes of this *Treason*, a Courtesie never mentioned to true *Traytors*, and a sufficient proofe that it was a religious fault that is soe easily cleared by a religious action. Yet we must with a iust Complaint of most vniust proceeding acknowledg, that at the barr, many things, wherof not so much as our thoughts were euer guilty, are, besides our Priesthood, partly by the Inditement, 30 partly by some in Office, layd to our Charge; and yet soe naked of proofes, or of any likely Coniectures, that we can never be Con-demned vpon any thing but our owne Confession of our Priesthood. And hereof the last Arraignement of three Priests at Westminster,[1] even since this Proclamation, gaue ample notice; wherin the Lord Chiefe Justice sayd, that though many things had bene vrged, yet

[1] *the last Arraignement of three Priests at Westminster.* On 4 December 1591 Edmund Jennings, Eustachius White, and Polydore Plasden were charged at Westminster with being seminary priests found within the realm contrary to the statute. They were found guilty and executed on 10 December.

he was to pronounce sentence of death against them only vpon that Statute of Comming into England being made Priests after the *Romane* order, since the first of her Maiesties Raigne. Yet it hath bene obiected somtymes against Priests, that they should pretend to kill your sacred person, a thing soe Contrary to their Calling, soe farr from their thoughts, soe voyd from all Pollicy, that whosoeuer will afford reason her right, cannot with reason thinke them soe foolish to wish, much lesse to worke such a thing, every way soe odious, noe way beneficiall. We come to shedd our owne, not
10 to seeke the effusion of others bloud. The weapons of our warrfare are spirituall, not offensive. We carry our desires soe high lifted aboue soe savage purposes, that we rather hope to make our owne Martyrdomes our steppes to a glorious eternity, then others deaths our purchase of eternall dishonour. And who but men vnwillinge to haue vs thought owners of our right witts, would abuse your Maiesties authority to sooth vp soe great vnlikelyhoods, sith none can be ignorant, how pernitious it were, both for Priests and all Catholiques to loose the protection of your Highnes, and to forgoe present sureties for vncertaine Changes. For if any would bequeath
20 his bloud to soe brutish a fact, if he were not as much enemy to all men as to himself, he would at the least haue some appearance of benefitt, that might be supposed to ensue to those, for whose good he would be thought to haue Cast away his life. But none that looketh but a stepp before him into future accidents, can thinke it any way availeable vnto vs to be bereaved of your Maiestie, sith our hopes are now bent, not vpon any expected happines, but only vpon a meere tolerable misery. And though our Case at this present be soe hard that it is in the next degree to extremity, yet we see things hange vpon soe doubtfull termes, that the death of
30 your Maiestie would be an Allarme to infinite vprores and likelier to breede all men a generall Calamity, then Catholiques any Cause of Comfort. And therfore for vs to seeke it, were not only an Impiety to our Cuntrie, but a tyranny to ourselues who of all others were surest to feele the fiercest Encounters of popular furie. And though we Could, as then noe man possiblie can, finde a private harbour from Common stormes; yet whom should we looke vpon, that may promise vs any hope of bettering our fortunes syth the likelyest to succeede are farther from Religion then your Maiestie ever was, and likelyer to Charge vs with a heavier hand, then to
40 lighten the burthen wherwith we are already brused. And both

your Maiesties sexe, inclined to pitty, and the mildnes of your owne disposition, rather wrested by others then prone of it self to angrie resolutions, maketh vs more willing to languish in this quartane of our lingring Combers[1] then to hazard our selues to those extreme fitts, that might happily be Caused by the heat of mens more warlike and lesse pittying mynds. For now our despairefull estate is much like a weak Castle besieged with enemies, and Continually battered with shott; in which though the abode be both dangerous and distressfull; yet without it there is nothing but certaine miserie. Rest you therfore assured (most gratious Soveraigne) syth we are devoted to soe hard a destiny, that we neither dare hope for any Cause of Contentment, nor end of our vnhappines, we had rather trust to the softnes of your mercifull hand, and next vnto god rest the height of our possibilities in your favour and Clemency, then by any vnnaturall violence against gods annoynted seeke the ruyne of our Realme, and draw vpon our selues the extreamest of worldly harmes. In this only we Craue admittance of our lowliest requests, that evill Informers robb not our words of due beliefe, nor draw your wisdome to their frivolous feares, wholly grounded in meere fictions, and purposely devised to our Ignominy.

10. Now wheras he imposeth on some to haue sayd, *That they would take part with any army of the Pope against our Realme*, it is a most vnlikely thing, vnles it were pressed out of some fraile tongue by force of torture, that was rather willing to say what they seemed to require then to abide the hell of soe intollerable torments. For such is now our forlorne estate, that we are not only Prisoners at every Promoters pleasure, and Common stepps of Contempt to tread vpon; but men soe neglected by our Superiours, and soe left to the rage of pittiles persons, that contrary to the Course of all Christian Lawes we are by the extreamest tortures forced to reveale our very thoughts. It is not enough to Confesse we are Priests, for that is seldome denied; but we must be vrged vpon the torture with other odious Interrogatories farr from our knowledg, much farther from our action: We are Compelled to accuse those whom our Conscience assureth vs to be Innocent, and to Cause their overthrowes by our Confessions, to whose soules we were Pastors, and they the Fosterers of our bodies; and if we doe not, because without vntruth or Iniury we cannot answere, we are soe vnmercifully tormented, that our deaths, though as full of panges as hanging drawing

[1] *Combers*. Troubles, distresses.

and vnbowelling vs quick can make them, are vnto vs rather remedies then further revenges, more releasing then increasing our miseries. Some are hanged by the hands, eight or nyne, or twelue howers together, till not only their witts, but even their sences faile them; and when the soule, weary of soe painfull an harbour, is ready to depart, they apply Cruell Comforts, and reviue vs, only to Martyr vs with more deaths; for eftsoones they hang vs in the same manner, tyring our eares with such questions, which either we cannot, because we know not, or without damning our soules we

10 may not satisfie. Some are whipped naked soe long and with such excesse, that our enemies vnwilling to giue Constancy her right name, sayd, that noe man without the help of the Divell could with such vndauntednes suffer soe much. Some, besides their tortures, haue bene forced to lie continually booted and Cloathed many weekes together, pined in their diett, Consumed with vermyne, and almost stifeled with stench. Some haue bene watched and kept from sleepe, till they were past the vse of reason, and then examined vpon the advantage, when they could scarcely giue accompt of their owne names. Some haue bene tortured in such parts, as is almost a torture

20 to Christian eares to heare it; let it then be iudged what it was to Chast and modest men to endure it, the shame being no lesse offensive to their mynds then the paine (though most excessiue) to their bodies. Divers haue bene throwne into vnsavourie and darke dungeons, and brought soe neere starvinge, that some for famine haue licked the very moisture of the walls; some haue soe farr bene Consumed that they were hardly recovered to life. What vnsufferable Agonies we haue bene put to vpon the Rack, it is not possible to expresse, the feeling soe farr exceedeth all speech. Some with Instruments haue bene rowled vp together like a ball, and soe

30 Crushed, that the bloud sprowted out at diuers parts of their bodies. To omitt divers other Cruelties, better knowne by their particuler names to the Rack-Masters and Executioners then to vs, though too well acquainted with the experience of their smarts: It is not possible to keep any reckoning of the ordinary punishments of Bridewell, now made the Common Purgatory of Priests and Catholiques, as grinding in the Mill, being beaten like slaves, and other outragious vsages. For to these are we forced at the discretion of such, as being to all other despised vnderlings, take a felicity in laying their Commaundements and shewing their authority vpon vs to whom

40 euery Warder, Porter, and Iaylor is an vnresisted Lord.

Thus (most exellent Princesse) are we vsed, yea thus are we most inhumanely abused, for being Priests, and of our Forefathers Faith; and of purpose to wring out of vs some odious speeches which may serue at our Arraignements for stales to the people to make them imagine greater matters then can be proved; wheras neither ill meaning, nor truth, but torture only was guide of the tongue that spake them, which in soe hard Conflicts of flesh and bloud, with soe bitter Convulsions, is apt to vtter any thing to abridge the sharpnes and severity of paine. Such vndoubtedly were the words alleaged of taking parte with any Army of the Popes against the Realme, if 10
ever they issued out of any Priests mouth: Or ells they were spoken by some vnskillfull Lay man, that not knowing how to answere such Captious questions, and for reverence to the Chiefe Pastor of gods Church, not daring to say he would fight against him, had rather venture his life by saying too much, then hazard his Conscience in not answering sufficient. But the Ignorance of one must not measure the meaninge of all, whom knowledg of our duties teacheth answeres farr different from this, and maketh vs ready to defend your Realme, as the Catholique subiects of your Maiesties Auncestors, or any other Prince were, are, or ever shalbe. For did 20
we Carry such trayterous mynds as our enemies giue out, we could not possiblie be soe Cowardlie or foolish as to suffer these tyrannyes for nothing, being otherwise resolved to die, and knowing the heads and hands from which these Cruelties proceede, without your Maiesties privitie. But as with patience and myldnes we hitherto haue, and hereafter meane to endure our scourges, having noe way deserved them but by seeking the salvation of soules, and praying for their good that torment vs: soe in answere of this point, we doe assure your Maiestie, that what Army soever should come against you, we will rather yeald our brests to be broached by our 30
Cuntrie swords, then vse our swords to th'effusion of our Cuntries bloud.

11. But let vs now Come to the Confession of some that should avouch *Cardinall Allen* to the Pope, and *Father Parsons to the King of Spaine to haue shewed certaine scrowles of the names of Catholiques, and to haue tempted them to renew the warr, by promising many thousands that should be in England ready to ayde them.* Concerning which there needeth no more to be sayd, but that the Penitents that made this Confession knew well enough they were not with their right ghostly Fathers, or ells they would neuer haue Committed such 40

a Sacriledge in abusing the Sacrament with such vntruthes. For we
are assured by their notice, who were more internall and Conversant
with them both, then the authors of this Confession euer could be,
that they are sufficiently informed of th'estate of Catholiques,
th'one by experience, th'other by continuall reports of those that
goe over; and therfore neither in pollicy, in which they are noe
Punies, nor in honesty, in which their Creditts doe lie, would they
deliuer such follies into Princes eares, which hearing by so many
Atturnies as all Potentates doe, were able to their face to disproue
them of falshood. For neither are the restraints and small nombers
of Catholiques soe seacrett, nor the Courses to suppresse them soe
vnknowne, but that euery Prince seeth an impossibility for them to
doe any thing, being (as before hath bene shewed) soe naked and
needie, and euery way soe vnprovided. Neither would they in
discretion, if they were (as they are not) the motioners of the Kings
Coming, feede him with a vaine hope of them, whom they at the
least know to be but a bundell of broken reeds, sith the more hellp
he expecteth the lesse he would bring, and happily build a maymed
plott vpon a false supposal, to his second ouerthrowe. And if his
preparations be greater then euer, why should he now trust more
vpon our lesse hability (the Lawes daily weakening our strength,
and the time howerly increasing his) then he did at his first assault,
when not any Priest or Catholique in *England* was acquainted with
his coming, or sure of his intent, till the common voice bruited it,
and our home provisions ascertained his purpose. And vnles they
were our enemies they would not in Common wisdome shew
scrowles of our names, or promise our assistance, sith they know
how ready our aduersaries at home would be vpon lesse matters to
seeke our subversion. Yea though they should (as we are sure they
would not) passe soe fond promises; yet could not Catholiques be
soe vnwise as to hazard all their estates in the vncertainty of forreyne
warr, seeing espetially his late ouerthrow, and knowing th'enterprise
to be such, that either the King of Spaine must stand vpon the
strength of his owne forces, or the sorry addition of their impotent
succour, which can neuer inable him to contriue his endeavours.
Finally both Cardinall Allen and Father Parsons are knowne generally to be men of excellent gifts, and noe such Novices in the knowledg of Princes Intelligence, as in the weighty points of alteration of
States and Invasion of Kingdomes, to presume to delude them with
impudent assertions, knowne to themselues to be false, as this

Informer acknowledgeth those to be. And if effects (the most infallible testimonies of intentions) may beare their deserved Credit against the naked and vnproved words of this partiall Inditor, Father Parsons hath by evident demonstrations of a loyall mynd sufficiently cleared himself from such vndue suspitions.[1] For having

[1] [*Persons in Spain.*] A fuller account of these events, which occurred in the winter of 1590–91, is to be found in the pamphlet, *Newes from Spayne and Holland*, 1593, at ff. 1b–2b. The pamphlet is in the form of a newsletter from a Dutchman who has recently been in England to a friend in London: '...so I ariued in Calliz of Andaluzia, by the end of Noueber, from whence passing within two or three dayes to the porte of S. Maries (which is but one or two howers sayling by water as you know) I had fitt occasion to informe my selfe very particularlie of the first pointe whereof we had hard so much in Ingland, and I promised to write you the truth to witt of the publique reconciling of so many Inglish Soldiars to the Catholique Romaine faith, as were at that tyme detayned prisoners in the Gallies of Spayne, which gallies commonly for the winter tyme doe reside in this porte of S. Maries as fittest of all Spayne for that purpose to resist the incursion of the moores. And for that this was the first matter wherof you and I talked and disputed so much in Ingland vppon the vncertaine relations that Souldiers brought vs thither from Spayne, you suspecting the matter to be feigned and I thinking the contrary: I shal first assure you in this that the whole hapned as we were informed, to witt, that aboue nyntie Inglish, partlie capteines, and officers and partlie marchaunts and commõ Souldiers, who had byn very resolute a long tyme in their religion, and had oftentymes affirmed to the Adelantado their general and other Captaynes and frendes which dealt with them in that behalf, that they would rather dye then relent therin, yet afterwardes vppon three or foure dayes cõference with an Inglish father or two of this side, they offered al most willingly to chainge their opinions and become catholiques,...and afterward al together in solemne procession were caried to the great church of the port, & there hard masse together, with extraordinary shew of contrition and repentance for the tyme past, & masse being ended, they al receaued the holy Sacrament of the aulter most deuoutly, & the Adelãtado with diuers other noble men knights and Captaines were communicated with them, for their comfort and deuotion: & that ended, the Adelantado (who is a most noble and honorable gentleman and affected exceedingly to the Catholiques of your nation) had them all home to his owne house, & gaue them a ryall dinner himselfe seruing them at the table, with *Don Iuan de Padilla* his eldest sonne, and heir, the marques of Montes Claros his nephew, *Don Iuan de Porto Carera* brother to the Earl of Palma his other nephew, *Don Iuan de Robles, Don Pedro de Acumnia*, & many other great men, who al did this honor to your nation that day, for ioy to see them so wilingly made Catholiques.'

This account, however, can scarcely be called unbiased, and Father Hicks believes that the author was none other than Persons himself ('Father Persons, S.J., and the Seminaries in Spain', *The Month*, CLVIII (1932), 26–35 at p. 29). There is little doubt that Father Hicks is right.

37

by his wisdome and rare parts purchased more then ordinary Credit
with the King of Spaine all that there haue bene eye witnesses of his
proceedings, can avouch, that he hath vsed the Kings favour euery
way to the benefitt, but noe way to the preiudice of your Maiesties
subiects. The soldiers that in your service lost their liberties, and
expected noe other entertainement but the Customary pay of professed hostility, were by his meanes and intercession, not only
pardoned their liues, but with new apparrell and money in their
purses enfranchised to their full liberty, either to stay in the Cuntry
if they soe fansied, or to returne to their owne, if they were soe
better pleased. Yea wheras by the long continued breaches betwene
Spaine and England the name of an Englishman was in most parts
of those Kingdomes farr lesse loved then knowne, he hath vsed such
meanes for the mitigation of their enmity towards vs, that we are
now noe lesse wellcome among them, and more Charitably vsed
then in most Nations: wherof not only the quiet of our Merchants,
the admittance of our students, even in the heart of the Realme (both
things vnvsuall in soe iealous and suspitious tymes) but the singuler
Curtesies towards their professed and knowne enemies, who were
actually taken in a violent enterprise against them, gaue proofe to
your Maiestie, witnessing how much Father Parsons hath qualified
the dislikes that warr bringeth forth. For even the Adalantado or
Chiefe gouernor of the gallies of Spaine to make manifest that
neither the King nor his Nobles had in the heat of their Martiall
broiles lost the feeling of their auntient League with our Cuntry,
sente into the gallies to our English Captiues the plate and meate
from his owne table, that the world might by his friendlines know,
how much better they can vse their enemies then some of your
Maiesties vnworthie Magistrates your naturall subiects and loyall
frends. And though it rest not in a private mans power to stay
th'endeavours of soe mighty a Prince, in so generall and important
an enterprise as his warr with *England* yet this without presumption
may be truly sayd, that if euer he should prevaile in that designement (as the Casualties of warr are most vncertaine to vs, and only
ouerruled by god) Father Parsons assisted with Cardinall Allens
authority, hath done that in our Cuntries behalf, for which his most
bitter enemies, and generally all your Maiesties subiects shall haue
cause to thanke him for his serviceable endeavours; soe farr hath
he enclined fury to Clemency, and rage to Compassion. The Confi-
tents therfore that gaue out these Confessions, did it but to sooth vp

such credulous Auditors, as they knew very apt to entertaine any rumors against the Creditt of Catholiques hoping of likelihood to sell them those Fables for some benefitt of more importance. Noe, noe (most gratious Soveraigne) it is not th'authority of two private men that can carry away such Princes soe readily to imploy their mayne forces, if they had not other motiues of greater Consequence. And who soe considereth our surprising of the Kings townes in Flaunders, our invading his Cuntries in Spaine and Portugall, our assisting his enemies against his daughters right in Brittany, our continuall and daily intercepting his treasure, warring with his Fleets, and annoying his Indies, shall finde other Causes of his comming since his last repulse then the slender hopes of a few beggered Catholikes, or the faint perswasion of two banished men.

12. It is also noe small Iniury that is offered to your Highnes in making your sacred hand, guided by such thoughts as scorne to haue vntruth the Patron of your actions, to seeme the Author of this sentence. *That many men of wealth professing in your Realme a contrary Religion are knowne not to be impeached for the same, either in their liues, lands, goods, or liberties, but only by paying a pecuniary somme, as a penalty for the tyme that they refuse to come to Church.* If this be as truly as confidently spoken, why were the venerable Prælates and other Priests and gentlemen deprived of their livings and pined in *Wisbiche*?[1] why were all the principall Catholiques committed at *Elie*, now to Ministers, then to *Banbury*, afterwards to their owne howses, with a short compasse about them, being now only lett loose to verifie a parte of this proclamation, and to be the easier ensnared in the perills therof, to which euery Child may see they are more subiect at home then they could be in prison. And if they Chaunce to be soe wary as not to be entrapped, effects will soone proue (if your Maiesties favor prevent not th'intentions of others) that this libertie was for a purpose, iust at the comming forth of the proclamation graunted, sith order will soone be taken, that they shall not surfett of being too long free. And if this saying be true, *that none are troubled for Religion*, what keepeth at this

---

[1] *Wisbiche.* Since about 1579 Wisbech Castle had been used for the confinement of some of the more influential priests, and by the time of the Armada there were about thirty-five in the Castle. It was here among the prisoners that the dissensions between the seculars and Jesuits first came to a head in 1595. The conditions of imprisonment in the Castle were far from stringent; see T. G. Law, *Jesuits and Seculars*, pp. xxxviii–xliii.

hower at *London, Yorke, Wisbiche,* and other places great nombers of many poore Catholiques in prison; some of which languishing away, with the incommodities of their enclosure, haue by a patient death obtained their best libertie; others yet, after many yeares in durance, for no other Cause but for their Religion, being offered liberty if they would goe to Church, pine still in a painfull restraint, witnessing to the world with their lingring miseries the manifest falsenes of this assertion. Was it not punishment for Religion, when a Company of honorable and worshipfull Ladies, and gentlewoemen
10 were most vncivilly lead through Cheapside, with their Priest before them, only for hearing Masse; and that before Priesthood was enacted to be Treason? Is not that very Statute a most heavy oppression, now, when the most of the few *Queene Mary* Fathers that are left, are become soe old and impotent, that they cannot possibly supply Catholiques spirituall necessities, to make it by Law Felony to receaue yonge Priests? Are not Catholiques shortened by these meanes from such helps, to which their Conscience and Religion bindeth them; a torment to vertuous mynds more afflictiue then any outward punishment? Are they not hereby tied to this
20 wounding and bitter Choise, either to liue like Heathens, without the Rites of all Christian and necessary Sacraments for their soules health, or to purchase them at the rigorous price of hazarding their liberties, liues, lands, and posterities, as in Case of Felony? In points also of our Credit, how deeply we are iniured in respect of our Religion, too many experiences make it most manifest. We are made the common Theame of euery railing declaimer; abused without meanes or hope of remedy, by euery wretch, with most infamous names. No tongue so forsworne but it is of credit against vs: None soe true but it is thought false in our defence. Our
30 sclaunders are common worke for idle presses; and our Creditts are daily solld at the Stationers stalls, every Libeller repayring his wants with impayring our honors, being sure that when all other matters faile, any Pamphlett against vs shalbe wellcomed with *Seene and allowed.* If we keep hospitality, we are Censured to be populer: If we forbeare it, we hoard vp money for seacrett purposes. If we be merry, we are fedd with forreigne hopes: If sadd, we are Malecontent with the state at home. If we subscribe to Articles, it must be called hypocrasie: If we refuse, disloyalty. In somme, we are measured by the eyes and tongues of such, whom we can no way
40 please but by being miserable. Yea the very name of a Catholique

or as they in their new stile terme it a Papist, is so knowne an advantage for euery one that either oweth them money or offereth them
Iniury, that they can neither clayme their rights, nor right their
wrongs, but their aduersaries straight leaving the mayne point,
pleadeth against them for their Recusancy; and thus trauersing[1]
their suits, often causeth their persons to be committed. If any
displeasing accident fall out, wherof the Authors are either vnknowne or ashamed, Catholiques are made common Fathers of
such infamous Orphanes, as though none were so fitt sluces as they,
to let out of euery mans sinke these vnsavoury reproaches. Not so   10
much but the Casuall Fiers[2] that somtimes happen in *London*; The
late vprores betwene the gentlemen and the Apprentices were layd
to our Charge, though th'occasioners of both were so well knowne,
that the report against vs could not but issue from an vndeserved
malice. Yea even *Hackett*,[3] a man so farr from our Faith as Infidelity
it self, and a little before so notorious a Puritane, that he was of
chiefe reckoning among them, when his blasphemies grew so great,
and his Articles so impious, that they made all Christian eares to
glowe, and his adherents to blush, then was he posted ouer to vs for
a Papist, and soe named to the vulgar sort: soe common a practise   20
it is to bestowe vpon vs th'infamies of all offenders. We omitt the
vnearned shame and contempt that the very Lawes lay vpon vs,
condemning the chiefe Functions of our Religion, partly for
treasonable, partly for otherwise punishable faults, and pretending
our auntient Faith, honoured in all former ages, to be soe detestable
a thing, that it should by a solemne Statute be thought necessary
to make it Treason to perswade any vnto it. We leave the sclaunders forged against Priests after their executions, purposely reserved
till the parties were past answering, and then devulged to make
them hatefull. It were infinite to lay before your Maiesties eyes all   30
the Crosses that in this kinde we beare, which to men whom either
gentrie or Nobility maketh tender ouer their honors, cannot but
be most bitter Corrasiues. For they neither dare revenge their owne
quarrells for feare of a double offence, to god, and to your Highnes,
nor hope for redresse by ordinary Courses: Soe farr hath disfavour

---

[1] *trauersing*. 'Traverse' is a legal term, meaning to make an affirmation
by way of contradicting a charge or allegation.

[2] *Casuall Fiers*. It will be recalled that even at the time of the Great Fire
of 1666 popular rumour laid the blame on the papists.

[3] *Hackett*. See note on p. 26, line 27 above.

excluded them from all needfull remedies. Yet must your Maiestie be informed (soe vncharitable are our enemies) that *we suffer nothing for Religion*, whom in respect only of Religion, these neglected miseries haue made most contemptible, euery one doing vs wrongs to please our superiours, whom they see careles in yealding vs any right. Now how vndutifull an Impeachment it was to the credit of your Maiesties words and writings, to publish vnder your soueraigne title, *that Catholiques for their Religion are not impeached in their goods or lands*, we leave it to effects to proue. And what is our Recusancy:
10 or Refusall to be presente at the protestants service, but a meere matter of Conscience? For as there is none soe knowne or vsuall a way to distinguish any Religion from other as th'externall Rites and Sacraments peculiar to euery one: soe can none more effectually deny his owne, then by making open profession of a contrary Faith, by his assistance and presence at the solemnities and service proper vnto it. For not only he that denieth Christ in his heart, but he also that denieth or is ashamed of him before men, shall in the later day be denied by him before his Angells. And seeing men best iudg of our mynds by our actions, we cannot possibly giue any better
20 proofe vnto them that we are noe Catholiques, then if we ioyne with protestants in their Churches and service; by which, as by their most certaine and espetiall markes, they themselues are knowne to be of that opinion. We therfore, not gainsaid in this by *Calvin*, *Melancthon*, or any other learned protestant, esteeme the voluntary presence of any man in or at the service of a Contrary Sect, a deniall of his Faith before men;[1] which being by Christ expresslie pro- hibited, cannot but be iudged a matter of meere Conscience and Religion; and as such a one it is by vs refused, sith neither pleasure nor Pollicy could otherwise with-holld vs, our Refusall redounding
30 to our soe great trouble and disadvantage. For first there are 20. pounds by the moneth[2] exacted of such as are able to pay it,

[1] *a deniall of his Faith before men*. In the earlier part of Elizabeth's reign Catholics had not hesitated to attend a sufficient number of Anglican services to meet the statutory requirements, but this practice was brought to an end by the Synod of Southwark, which met under Persons and Campion in 1580. It was then ruled that 'So public an act as is going to the church, where profession is made to impugn the truth and to deface, alienate and bring into hatred Christ's Catholic Church, is the highest iniquity that can be committed.'

[2] *20. pounds by the moneth*. The fine exacted of recusants for not attending church.

after the rate of 13. moneths by the yeare (an account vnvsuall in all other Causes) as the Lawes commonly read, printed, and practised doe witnes. And multitudes of the vnabler sort of Catholiques daily feele, that all their goods and two third parts of their lands[1] are seized on for their Recusancy, that cannot yearly pay 13. score pounds for the same. And this is both prescribed and performed with such rigor, that it is in the Leases by a spetiall proviso ordained, that Recusants should not be so much as Tenants to their owne lands: soe severely is our Religion punished in that behalfe. Yea and this Law hath bene so violently executed, that where poore Farmers 10 and Husbandmen had but one Cow for themselues and many Children to live vpon, that for their Recusancy hath bene taken from them. And where both Kine and Cattell were wanting, they haue taken their Coverletts, sheetes, and blanquetts from their bedds, their victualls and poore provision from their howses, not sparing so much as the very glasse of their windowes, when they found nothing ells to serve their turnes withall; with all which most pittifull vsage the poore soules both in the North and other Cuntries haue bene continually cumbred, noe Complaints taking place, where these outrages were rather commended for good services, then 20 rebuked for misdemeanors; soe irrecoverably are we condemned to a most servile bondage. And if your Maiestie did but know what other extreme penury and desolation they ordinarily feele, your mercifull heart (neuer hardened to soe lamentable spoiles) would rather haue the Lawes repealed then th'execution soe intollerable. It is not possible to expresse in words the continuall hell we suffer by the merciles searching and storming of Pursevants and such needy Officers, that Care not by whose fall they rise, not having any deserts or other degrees to Clymbe to the height of their Ambition, but the punishments and paines of poore Catholiques. 30 They water their fortunes with the showers of our tenderest vaines, and build their howses with the ruynes of ours, tempering the morter of their foundations with our Innocent bloud. Our Livings are but snares for the owners lives, commonly made the Fee of euery mercinary mouth that can by sounding our disgraces into credulous eares, procure themselues warrants to seaze vpon our

---

[1] *all their goods and two third parts of their lands.* This confiscation was the penalty for non-payment of the fines for refusing to attend church. Both the fine and the penalty were fixed by a Statute of 1585, passed at the same time as the other which made it treason for a priest to enter the realm.

substance. They make our Wills before we be sick, bequeathing to their owne vses what share they like, and by displanting of our offspring adopt themselues to be heires of our Lands, begging and broking for them, as if either we were condemned for fooles, or in a perpetuall Minority. And not contented with our wealth, they prosecute our lives, neuer thinking their possession sure, till th'assurance be sealed with our death: soe easy it is for our enemies to quench their angry thirst in our bloud. Yea we are made soe common forrage for all hungry Cattell, that even the thieues, with scutchions[1] and Counterfeit warrants, haue vnder the pretence of Pursevants, spoiled vs in our howses, having th'officers to assist them in the Robberies; soe ready they are at euery ones call to practise their authority to our vexation: and so well knowne it is to euery way beater how open all Catholiques lie to the pray. And though some few finde more favour, being able to follow it with golden Petitions, yet all the rest, whose meaner estates cannot reach the Charge of such Costly Friends, are made common lotts, open to euery Chance in the dice, to giue entrie to their aduersaries by their dispatching, their owne servants and tenants Crowing ouer them, and vaunting that euery Pawne may giue the Mate to their highest Fortunes. For be he neuer so base that plaieth with them, vpon the least advantage he is sure of many that will back him in it, and heaue his trick[2] with a sure help, though it be the Sonne that taketh against his owne Parents, or any faulty drudg that for feare of due correction accuseth his Master. It were infinite to sett downe the Laborinth of our afflictions, in which what way soeuer we goe, it is but a loosing of our selues, and a winding vs further into an endles course of Calamities. Let this suffice, that so heavy is now the hand of our Superiors against vs, that we are generally accounted men whom it is a credit to pursue, a disgrace to protect, a commodity to spoile, a gaine to torture, a glory to kill. We presume that your Maiestie seldome or neuer heareth the truth of our persecutions, your lenity and tendernes being knowne to be soe professed an enemy to these Cruelties, that you would neuer permitt their Continuance, if they were expressed to your Highnes as they are practised vpon vs. Yet sith we can bring the ruyne of our howses, the Consumption of our goods, the pouerty of our estates, and the

---

[1] *scutchions.* The badge worn on the breast by pursuivants in their capacity as officers of the courts.

[2] *heave his trick.* 'Heave' in thieves' cant meant to 'lift' or rob.

weeping eyes of our desolate Families for the palpable witnesses of the truth of these Complaints; let vs not be so farr exiled out of the limitts of all Compassion, as besides all other evills, to haue it confirmed vnder your Maiesties hand, *that we suffer no punishments for Religion*, suffering in proofe all punishments for nothing ells. We haue bene long enough cutt of from all Comfort, and stinted to an endles taske of sorrowes, growing in griefs as we grow in yeares, one misery ouertaking another, as if euery one were but an earnest for a harder payment. We had some small hope, that our continued patience, and quiet effusion of our bloud at your Maiesties feete, would haue kindled some sparkle of remorse towards vs: But still we see that we are not yet sunke to the depth of our misfortunes. We must yet tread the restles Maze of new aggreivances, sith we perceaue by this proclamation, that our Case is soe farr of from being pitied, that it is not so much as knowne where it can only be redressed. Yet sith help neuer cometh to late to soe helples Creatures, who daily are drawen nearer to the brinke of a generall destruction, which some that giue ayme to your Maiestie seeme willing that you should discharge vpon vs: We are forced to divulge our Petitions, and by many mouthes to open vnto your Highnes our humble suites. For neither daring our selues to present them in person, being terrified with the president of his Imprisonment that last attempted it,[1] nor having the favour of any such Patron, as would be willing to make himself Mediator to your Maiestie, we are forced to committ it to the multitude, hoping that among soe many as shall peruse this short and true Relation of our troubles, god will touch some mercifull heart to let your Highnes vnderstand th'extremity of them; which if we were once sure to haue bene effectually performed, we might either sett vp our rest in an vnflexible sentence of misery, which we hope will neuer proceede from so easy and gratious a Iudg as your sacred self, or rather expect some lenitiue to allay the anger of our smart, a thing more incident to the myld temper of soe exellent a mynde. In the meane time, we humbly craue pardon of this enforced defence and necessary Supplication, which was extracted from vs by open and vnsupportable vntruthes, noe lesse needfull for your Maiestie to know, then for vs to disproue, implying the vndeserued touch of your Highnes word,

---

[1] *the president of his Imprisonment that last attempted it.* A reference to Richard Shelley and the petition he presented to the Queen on behalf of the Catholics on 15 March 1585. See further Appendix III.

and playning the direct path to our intended subuersion. Accept it therfore (most mercifull Princesse) and all our humble duties and sureties with it, which with most loyall thoughts and serviceable resolutions are vnfeynedlie betrothed to your Maiesties defence.

God of his infinite goodnes prosper and preserue you to his glory, your Subiects Comfort, and your owne both temporall and eternall happines. This last of December.

Finis.

THE TEXTS

The *Humble Supplication* has survived in the following texts:

1. Petyt MS. 538.36 in the Library of the Inner Temple. Small folio, $11\frac{1}{2} \times 7\frac{1}{4}$ inches.

The greater part of this volume, which contains a number of Catholic tracts, consists of transcripts in the same hand, a cursive secretary hand with no special pretence to elegance. The *Humble Supplication* occupies ff. 56–77.
Begins: 'The Coppy of an humble Supplication to her Matie in answere to the late Proclamation.'
Ends: 'This last of December. | ffinis.'

2. Petyt MS. 538.10 in the Library of the Inner Temple. Folio.

Ff. 129–140 consist of a transcript of the *Humble Supplication* on paper $13 \times 8\frac{1}{2}$ inches, though of a size somewhat smaller than that found in the rest of the volume. It is written in a formal secretary hand, with a very sparse use of italics, and is apparently the work of a professional scribe.
Begins: 'An humble supplication to her Matie | 1595.'
Ends: 'December. 14. | Anno. 1595 | Finis |'.

3. MS. Ellesmere 2089, in the Henry E. Huntington Library, San Marino, California. Quarto, unbound.

This manuscript has been detached from a bound collection of tracts, in which it was no. 8. It consists of 28 leaves, with borders ruled in red, and the text occupies ff. 1–26. It is carefully written in a secretary hand, with a sparse use of italics, and was presumably made by a professional scribe for Sir Thomas Egerton.
Begins: 'An humble Supplication to her Matie in aunswere of a late Proclamation.'
Ends: 'Finis December 31. A°/1592.'

4. Edition of 1600 (*S.T.C.* 7586).

[Within a rule within a border of type ornaments] AN | HVMBLE | SVPPLICATION | *TO HER MA-* | IESTIE. | ✠ | [rule] | [type ornament] | [rule] | [rule] | *Printed, Anno Do.* 1595.
Octavo. Five and a half sheets: A–E⁸, F⁴. A1, title; A2, beginning of text; F 4ᵛ, text ends, '*December* 14. Anno. 1595. FINIS.' A2 is page 1, and pages are numbered 1–86; the numbers on pp. 44 and 45 are interchanged, and p. 68 is misnumbered 88. The year in the date on the title-page and at the end is, of course, a deliberate falsification.

Recorded copies: British Museum, shelf-mark 3935.aa.33; Lambeth Palace, 2 copies, shelf-marks XXXI.9.b(3) and A.4.13.f(2); Stonyhurst College; Cashel Cathedral; the Rev. L. Hicks, S.J. Another copy was offered for sale several years ago by Messrs Quaritch, in their catalogue no. 436.

The British Museum copy has been carefully corrected in manuscript in two contemporary hands. The first, a secretary hand, appears up to p. 40, and the second, an italian hand, on pp. 42–64. There are no corrections in the last quarter of the book.

There seem to be two clearly distinguishable textual traditions: the one represented by the octavo (O) and Petyt 538.10 (B), the other by Petyt 538.36 (A) and the Ellesmere MS. (E). O and B, however, show such consistently close agreement that it is impossible to avoid the conclusion that B is merely a transcript of the printed edition, and that its few variants have no independent textual authority. They have therefore been ignored in the collations which follow.

I am inclined to believe that the day and month (though not, of course, the year) at the end of O are reliable, and that this version goes back to the author's first draft. A and E, on the other hand, are dated seventeen days later, and are presumably descended from a later version. Some of the differences between the two textual groups suggest author's revisions, especially those recorded in the notes to pp. 28–29, 32–36, where there seems to have been a genuine attempt to eliminate redundancies of expression.

Both A and the British Museum copy of O have been elaborately corrected, A by the original scribe. The interesting feature of these corrections is that each has been corrected from an exemplar of the other textual group. In the British Museum copy the corrections are always an improvement, but those in A are sometimes palpably wrong.

E, though fairly closely allied to A, is at once more calligraphic and more careless. It possesses one feature that separates it from the other texts: in the account of the Babington conspiracy (pp. 16–25) the responsibility for certain acts is differently attributed. Why this should have been so I cannot say; but in each instance E is wrong.

A is the better of the two representatives of the second, revised, version of the text, and some of the reasons for choosing it as copy-text in preference to E are stated very briefly in the note on p. xxiv. A is, of course, a conflated text, but since all the corrections made in it can be observed and recorded, it is possible without difficulty to reconstruct its uncorrected state. The frequency with which E and O agree against A in unessential readings, which do not seriously affect the sense, suggests that the scribe of A, however intelligent and careful he may have been, did not always follow his original with complete accuracy.

The textual notes that follow do not attempt to record every variant; they represent only a selection from a much longer list. They do, however, try to record every departure from the readings of the copy-text; all the corrections introduced into A and the British Museum copy of O; such readings as suggest revision; such other variants as materially affect the sense; and a selection of further variants to illustrate the relationships between the various texts.

TEXTUAL NOTES

A Petyt MS. 538.36
E MS. Ellesmere 2089
O the octavo edition
M manuscript corrections in the British Museum copy of *O*
cor. M after the citation of a reading from *O* indicates that the corrected
reading is the same as that adopted in the present text

PAGE I

title The Coppy of an...*A*; in aunswere of a...*E*; in answere...Proclamation
om. O.   **6**   Princes] Princesse *E.*   **8**   to] *cor. fr.* of *A.*   **9**   place] rometh *E*,
roome *O.*   person] presence *E.*   **10**   Arbiter] arbitrator *O.*   **11**   meane-
nesse] *cor. to* meanes *A*; meanes *E, O.*   **13**   vertues] *cor. fr.* duties *A*; duties *E, O.*
14   last] iust *O.*   **25**   your] yea euen the *E.*   **27**   vntruths] truthes *O, cor. M.*
soe] *cor. fr.* the *A.*   **28**   title] sight *O*; stile *E, M.*   **30**   any] *om. E.*

PAGE 2

2   abused] abased *E, O; cor. M.*   **3**   Magistrates] magistracye *E.*   must]
so E; most *A, O.*   **5**   knowledg] *cor. fr.* notice *A*; notice *E.*   but be] *cor. to*
be but *A*; but bee *E.*   **10**   that this is] this to be *O.*   **11**   who] *cor. fr.* w^ch *A*;
w^ch *E.*   **13**   shrowdes] shadowes *O, cor. M.*   **14**   beare] bare *E, O.*   **15**   beleife]
so E, M; reliefe *A, O.*   **20**   Clamerous] *cor. fr.* Declaymers *A*; declamers *E*;
declamorous *O.*   **21**   be] to *deleted before* be *A.*   **23**   their] *added above the
line in A; om. E.*   **24**   rather then] *cor. fr.* rather to...will, then *A.*   **25**   whome]
so E; when *A, O.*   **28**   to be] *added above the line in A.*   **29**   to] *cor. fr.* of *A*;
of *E.*   mynds] *cor. fr.* view *A*; viewes *E; cor. to* viewe *M.*   **31**   nearly] *cor. to*
meerly *A.*   **32**   mens] *inserted in A; om. E.*

PAGE 3

2   to] *cor. fr.* vnto *A.*   **8**   the] *cor. fr.* that *A*; that *E.*   termes] *cor. fr.* name *A*;
name *E, O.*   **9**   often and generally] *cor. fr.* generally & often *A*; generally and
often *E.*   **12**   owne] *so E*; name *cor. fr.* ffaith *A.*   **13**   in the Vniuersity...
studies] *om. O*; vniuersities *E.*   **15**   troubled] *inserted above the line in A.*   **21**   in
forsaking that] *cor. fr.* & to forsake *A*; to forsake the *E.*   **27**   what] *cor. fr.*
that *A*; that *E.*   **29**   vpon] in *O*, on *M.*   **32**   fidelity] *cor. fr.* ffelicity *A*;
felicitye *E.*   worthier] *cor. fr.* worthye *A.*   **34**   engage] *cor. fr.* to engage *A*;
to engage *E.*   greatest] great *O, cor. M.*   **36**   price] *cor. fr.* prize *A*; prices *E.*
infernall paine] *cor. fr.* a condemning pardon *A*; a condemning pardon *E.*

PAGE 4

1   if] *inserted in A; om. E.*   seeke with] seeke yt w^th *E.*   **3**   we thinke that we
owe] *cor. fr.* wherin we thinke we shew *A*; showe *E, M.*   **8**   by an] an
inserted in A; w^th *E.*   **9**   on] *cor. fr.* of *A.*   **20**   our] *om. O, inserted M.*
21   ground] *om. O, inserted M.*   **23**   make] *cor. fr.* making *A.*   **28**   happely]
om. E.   to be] *cor. fr.* by of *A*; by *E.*   **32**   either] *inserted in A.*

AGE 5

Cause] Case *E*, *O*.   **3** home] is more lamentable *deleted after this word in A*
amentable] miserable *O*.   **4** any] *inserted in A*; *om. E*. chosen] *cor. fr.*
hese *A*; these *E*.   **13** calmer] calme *O*, *cor. M*. perfected] proffited *E*.
7 this Penners] their pennes *E*.   **22** truly be] truly *inserted in A*; bee truly *E*.
vowed] auoided *O*; auowched *M*.   **25** rare] *cor. fr.* owne *A*.   **27** seconded]
ecunded *O*, *cor. M*.   **28** as] *om. O*, *cor. M*. leave] it *deleted after this word in*
4; yt *E*.   **30** noe] we *O*, *cor. M*.

AGE 6

worthines] *cor. fr.* worth *A*.   **8** the 14. his] *inserted in A*; *om. E*.   **10**
noweth] is ignorāt of *O*. that] of *O*, *cor. M*.   **13** endeavours] endevour *E*;
dventures *O*, *cor. M*.   **14** and] to *deleted after this word in A*.   **17** soe] *cor.*
r. such *A*. soe forcible and mightie] so mightie *O*, *cor. to* so forcible *M*.
0 highest] *cor. fr.* height *A*. his] *inserted in A*.   **22** but...afforde] but that
hey are able *added in A*. were able] *so E*, *O*.

AGE 7

if...dignities] *om. O*.   **2** a way] a *inserted in A*; weighe *E*.   **4** his...
esse] *om. O*.   **6** simpler] simple *O*, *cor. M*.   **7** sort] *inserted in A*.   **10** both]
nserted in A.   **12** may] *inserted above the line in A*.   **15** tenth] *altered from*
Tithes *in A*.   **18** multitude] *altered from* company *in A*.   **20** For...Realme]
m. E.   **21** out] *inserted in A*.   **23** soile] Countrie *O*, *cor. M*.   **26** in] *altered*
rom an *in A*; an *E*.   **28** of] *om. O*, *cor. M*. soe] *inserted in A*. dissolute]
lesolute *O*, *cor. M*.   **29** Causes] occasions *E*; actions *O*, *cor. M*. dis-
olutenes] *altered from* dissolution *in A*; dissolution *E*, *M*.

AGE 8

happely it may be imagined that we say] yt maye happily bee conceaued,
hat wee imagine *E*. imagined] *cor. fr.* conceaved *in A*. say] *cor. fr.* imagine
n *A*.   **6** College] *altered from* Colleges *A*; Colledges *E*.   **11** our returnes]
or. fr. home *A*; retourne *E*.   **15** bloudy] dreadfull *E*; *om. O*.   **23** suteth]
eemeth *O*, *cor. M*. Calling] *so E*, *O*; Callings *A*.   **27** it] *inserted in A*;
m. E.

AGE 9

weighty] mighty *O*.   **2** our] *cor. fr.* one *A*.   **11** youthly] youthful *E*, *O*.
resses] tresses *E*.   **12** disguising] disguisage *O*.   **14** vanity] beautie *O*,
or. M.   **15** shrowded] *cor. to* shadowed *A*; shadowed *O*, *cor. M*.   **16** if]
he *deleted after this word in A*; if the *E*.   **17** Ministeries] *cor. to* Ministers *A*;
Ministers *O*, *cor. M*; miseryes *E*.   **33** accepted] excepted *E*, *O*; *cor. M*.
5 patience] *altered to* passions *A*; passions *O*, *cor. M*. possession] *so E*;
ossessions *A*, *O*.

PAGE 10

lack] want *O*.   **5** most] *inserted in A*. wher] *cor. fr.* wherin *A*; wherein
E.   **7** hired] *cor. fr.* hard *A*. Or] *inserted in A*; *om. E*.   **9** posterities] *so*
E, *O*; prosperities *A*.   **14** more] *cor. fr.* nearer *A*; nearer *E*. leave] left *E*, *O*.

18 needed to] needed not to *E, O.* **20** to haue risen] *cor. fr.* to rise *A*; to rise *E, M.* **21** preheminence] *cor. fr.* preferment *A*; preheminencie *O.* omitt] remitte *O, cor. M.* had] haue *O, cor. M.* **22** Alliance] allowance *O, cor. M.* **25** displeasing] displeasuring *E.* **32** inditements] *so O*; inducements *A, E.* **34** in] *so E, O*; to *A.*

PAGE II

1 obloquy] oblique *O, cor. M.* **6** could...notice] *om. E.* **9** and...haue] And as for the rest, which are of riper yeares they haue *O.* **10** notefied for] noticed of *E.* **12** vnproued] vnapproued *E*; approued *O, cor. M.* **17** rebate] *so E, M*; relate *A, O.* dint] *altered to* doubt *A*; doubt *O, cor. M.* **18** pointed] *altered to* ioynd *A*; ioyned *O, cor. M.* **21** humblye] humbye *A.* right] *altered from* beleefe *A.* **25** for witnesses] to witnesse *O.* **34** may be] *altered from* wilbe *A.*

PAGE 12

4 such] selfe *O.* **10** bottomles] *altered to* booteles *then back to* bottomles *A.* **11** many soe] soe *added in A*; many, and so *O.* **13** death] *om. E, O.* an] *om. E, O.* **14** enemies could] enemy would *E, O.* **16** can] *altered from* could *A*; could *E.* **19** in] *altered from* of *A.* **20** accomplish] doe *O.* **28** as] *inserted in A before* hard. **30** knowne] *altered from* great *A.* **31** more] farre more *E.* **34** pollitique] publike *O.* **37** ells] *inserted in A.* but] of *deleted after this word in A.*

PAGE 13

1 but] then *E.* **2** wrastling with] wresting for *O.* **3** a] *altered from* the *A.* **4** over] *cor. fr.* of *A.* And] *inserted in A*; *om. E, M.* **5** feigneth] findeth *O, cor. M.* **8** obtaine] attaine *E, O.* **19** vs from the] vs; the *E.* **24** reckon] recount *O.* **26** displacing] displeasing *O.* **28** perfected] proffited *E.* **30** contemned] contented *O, cor. M.* **31** anothers] any others *E.* **32** effusion] affection *O, cor. M*; to *deleted after this word in A.*

PAGE 14

5 our bodies] o^r whole body *E.* bodies...excellent] bodies: for the first, give then (O most gratious *O.* **7** iniurious] enuious *O.* durst] *inserted above the line in A.* **11** come] *cor. fr.* Campe *in A.* **13** your Highnes, or] their Princes highnes, and *O.* **14** power or assistance to the Spanish] powers to the Spanish Princes *O.* **19** Incumbents] incombences *O, cor. M.* **20** both] *inserted above the line in A.* **22** all] *inserted above the line in A.* fancies] phantasies *E, O.* **23** muddy] madd *M.* **25** expose] offer *E, O.* **26** and] *cor. fr.* yea *A*; yea *E.* most] *om. E, O.* **28** any] *om. E, O.* **31** occurences] occurrentes *E*, accurrants *O.* **35** Cause] case *O.*

PAGE 15

2 mutening] mutinye *E.* **9** vntrue] *om. E.* surmises] surmisers *A.* **18** and but] *om. E, O*; *underlined for omission in A.* **19** restrained] refrained *E.* nature, it] nature. It *E, O.* **22** the] *inserted in A*; *om. E.* withhelld] hath helde *O, cor. M.* **23** would] could *E, O*; *cor. M.* **24** soe

ill mynded] of ill mind *O*.　then live only] then to liue *O*.　**26** them]
inserted above the line in A.　**27** gentleman] *cor. fr.* gentlemen *in A*; Gentlemen *E*.　**29** mannerles] manerleste *O*; mercilesse *M*.

3 authority] submiss *deleted before this word in A*.　**8** most] *inserted above the
line in A*.　**10** willing] *cor. fr.* will *in A*.　**13** flint-harted] flintyharted *E*.
14 sparkles] sparkes *O*.　his] their *O, cor. M*.　the] *inserted above the line after
of in A*.　**15** that] like *O, cor. M*.　**19** Father] and *inserted above the line
after this word in A*.　**20** all ages] allegiance *O, cor. M*.　**25** as] *om. E; so O,
cor. M*.　submitted] submissiue *E*.　**27** Case] Cause *E*.　vnveyled] vnsound
O, cor. M.　**28** mirror] error *M*.　**31** then to keep vs] *om. O, cor. M*.
34 when] *cor. fr.* whom *in A*; whome *E*.　**35** vs] *inserted above the line in A*;
om. E.　in] *inserted above the line in A*; *om. E*.　**36** other] *inserted above the
line in A*.

1 Ballard and] and *cor. fr.* or *in A*.　**3** nyne] *marked for deletion in A*; *om.
O, cor. M*.　**4** Chronicle] cor. fr. Chronicler in A.　**5** 33.] *cor. to* 35. *in A*;
35. *O*.　**7** their Consciences] Conscience *E, O*.　**8** five] *so E*; few *A, O*.
9 in life or action professed himself to be] action *cor. fr.* actions *in A*; nor
Actions *E*; himself *om. E*; professed in life, nor action to be *O*.　**11** in] *cor.
fr.* by *in A*.　**13** motives] mutinies *O*.　**16** in truth] *om. O, cor. M*.　snare
to entrap] *altered from* gynne to ensnare *in A*; gynne to ensnare *E*.

3 Poolie] Poole *here and elsewhere in E*.　Sir Francis Walsinghams] M^r
Secretaries *E*.　**4** Masters] M^r his *E*.　**7** hookes] *cor. fr.* hopes *in A*; hopes *E*.
11 Masters] M^r his *E*.　**22** vnchristian] Christian *E, O*.　**23** Decipherers]
decipherer of y^e *E*; deciphers *O, cor. M*.

3 owne] *om. O, cor. M*.　**4** and fewell] *om. O, cor. M*.　**5** be] *altered from*
doe *in A*.　sacrificed] the sacrifice *E, M*.　since, it is knowne] sure it is, *O*.
8 Sir Francis his] Sir Frauncis Walsinghams *E, O*.　having...before bene]
cor. fr. having bene...before *in A*.　**9** Master Secretaries] S^r ffrauncis *E*.
Philips] Phillips his *E*.　**10** on foote] *cor. fr.* a floate *in A*; a floote *E*.　**15**
tenor] tenure *E*.　**16** to...to] *cor. fr.* by...by *in A*.　**17** which was]
wheras *O, cor. M*.　**19** Sir Francis Walsinghams] Mr Secretaries *E*.　priuie]
private *O*.　**20** further] priuie *O*.　to] th *deleted before this word in A*.　**21**
proceedings] proceeding *E*.　French] *om. E*.　**22** Chatteneufe] *cor. to*
Cateneufe *in the margin of A*; Shateneus *E*; Catanense *O*.　then] *inserted above
the line in A*.　**23** Queene of Scotts] Scottish Queene *E, O*.　**24** accounted]
om. E, O.　**27** his] the *O, cor. M*.　**28** parte] great part *O, cor. M*.　**29**
that] *cor. fr.* the *in A*.　in] *inserted above the line in A*; *om. E*.　**30** thev]
inserted above the line in A.　**31** being] *marked for omission in A*; *om. O,
cor. M*.　bad] good *E*.　in] by *O, cor. M*.

PAGE 20

6 infortunate] *om. E*; vnfortunate *O*.   **14** were] *cor. fr.* was *in A*.   **16** owne] *marked for omission in A; om. O*.   Secretaries] Secretary Walsinghams *E*.   **17** Correspondencye] *cor. to* Correspondent *in A*; correspondent *O*.   **19** Queene of Scotts] Scottish Queene *E*.   **20** this designement] their designementes *E*.   **21** motions] *cor. fr.* matters *in A*.   **23** that she] they *O, cor. to* she *M*.   **24** Mistress] Maister *O, cor. M*.   **26** Secretary] Gifforde *E*.   **29** Poolie] Phillipps *E*.   **30** his taske] the matter *O*.   Ballard and the gentlemen] *cor. fr.* the gentlemen & Ballard *in A*; the Gentlemen, and Ballard *E*.   **35** Conster] consture *O*.

PAGE 21

2 offers] Officers *O*, offerer *M*.   **4** Covine] *cor. to* cunning *in A*; Coven *E*, cŭning *O*.   **7** Queene of Scotts] Scottish Queene *E*.   **8** Poolie] Phillipps *E*.   **9** Secretarie] Secretarye Walsingham *E*.   **10** Queenes] Scottish Queene *E*.   Sir Francis Walsinghams] Mʳ Secretaryes *E*.   **12** Naw and Curle] Maw & Curle *with* Nato and Curlie *added in the margin in A*; Nato and Curlie *O*; Nato *cor. to* Nawe *M*.   **13** the ditty of] *om. O*.   ditty] dyet *E*.   Ryme] tyme *E, O*.   **15** Gifford] Gilbert *E*.   **17** Nawe] Mawe *A*; Nato *O, cor. M*.   Curle] Curlie *O*.   boulstred with soe large] boulstred out wᵗʰ so many larg *E*.   **19** away] *added above the line in A; om. E; deleted M*.   Bernard] Barnardye *E*.   Mawde] *deleted in A*; made *O*; Mendosa *E*.   **20** vndoubted] *cor. fr.* redoubted *in A*.   with Ballard] *om. O*.   **25** Sir Francis Walsingham] Mʳ Secretary Wal: *E*.   nomber] manner *O*.   **28** wound in] wonne in *E*; wonne *O*.   **29** man] men *O, cor. M*.   **30** occasion] *cor. fr.* occasioner *A*.   **33** with] *cor. fr.* of *in A*; of *E*.

PAGE 22

1 the] *inserted above the line in A*.   **5** motioner] motion *O*; cheif moticioner *E*.   **6** Secretary] Secretarie Wal: *E*.   **8** a] *inserted above the line in A*.   **12** Sir Francis] Mʳ Secretary *E*.   **13** tyme wherin] the tyme when *E*.   **19** heare] *cor. fr.* see *in A*; see *E*.   **21** watched...eares] watched, hewes & Cryes raisd, infinite howses searched, frights bruted, the peoples eares *E*.   **25** kindling] building *O*.   **28** all] *inserted above the line in A*.   **29** haunts] hearts *O, cor. M*.   **30** the] *cor. fr.* a *in A*.   **31** forsooth] *inserted above the line in A*.

PAGE 23

6 Queene of Scotts] Scottish Queene *E*.   **8** Polies] Phillips his *E*.   the] *underlined for omission in A; om. O*.   **10** Secretary] Secretary Wal: *E*.   **11** dimme] *cor. fr.* weake *in A*; to weake *E*; diuine *O cor. M*.   **17** Proviso] promise *O, cor. M*.   **21** Monarchie] Kingdome *E, O*.   **24** Credit] credit for such a matter *O*.   **29** men] *cor. fr.* them *in A*.   **31** flying] fliting *O*.   Reports] *om. E, O*.   **32** without the] out the *inserted above the line in A*.   such] *inserted here above the line in A, and deleted before* shipps.   **33** in] *cor. fr.* at *in A*; at *E*.   **34** ouersight] sight *O, cor. M*.   **37** effect] effectuate *with last four letters underlined for deletion in A*.   which] *so E; om. A, O*.

PAGE 24

1 we] *cor. fr.* I in *A*. 2 any] *inserted above the line in A*. 10 an] any *E*.
11 declared] *cor. fr.* declaymed *in A*. 12 as] *om. O, cor. M*. for] *so E*;
from *A*. could] *om. O, cor. M*. first come] runne first *O*. 14 their] her
O, cor. M. to] *inserted above the line in A*. 21 violently] *cor. fr.* vehemently
in A. 22 holld] heed *O, cor. M*. 24 full] *word uncertain in A, and marked
for deletion*. 28 Secretaryes] Secretarie Walsingham *E*. 29 Spies Cosening]
Spies, Cosoninge *E*.

PAGE 25

2 effect] officer *O, cor. M*. assistance] assistants *O*. 4 way] *so E, O*;
one *A*. 5 away] *inserted above the line in A*; *om. E*. his] the *O, cor. M*.
11 Challenge] chalenging *O*. 12 a promise] promised *O*, promise *M*.
Prince] king *O*. 15 this] that *E*, their *O*. 20 (most] much *O, cor. M*.
24 heaviest] *om. E*, heauie *O*. 25 meanes] wayes *O*. their] *inserted above
the line in A*; *om. E*. 26 violenting] wresting *E*. to evill by these] too euilly;
by these *O*; euill *M*. 27 be free from] be, from *O, cor. M*. 28 bounding]
binding *O*. 33 other] *inserted above the line in A*. 37 fore-arme] for
arming *E*; so arme *O*. 39 motion] motiue *E*.

PAGE 26

2 way] weigh *O*. vnto] into *E, O*. 9 in trayning vs] to drawe vs *O*.
12 found] wonne *E, O*. 13 therfore] *a second* therfor *deleted after this word
in A*. 16 ariving] arising *E*. 21 their] the *O, cor. M*. 23 estate] State *E*.
24 soone] seeme to *O*. 28 Messias] *cor. fr.* godhead *A*. 31 of scourges]
of oʳ scourges *E*; of your scourges *O*. 32 out] not *O, deleted M*. Concealed]
conceaued *E*. 34 wreake] *written above* weake *or* wreake *deleted in A*.

PAGE 27

2 open offer to an] open offer of *O, cor. to* made open offer of *M*.
5 Abettors] bearers *O, cor. M*. touched] charged *O*. 21 esteemed so]
so esteemed for *O*. 24 can there move] then can moue *E, O*. 29 it is]
that *deleted before it in A*. 30 well being] *cor. to* well doing *in A*; wel-doing *O*.
35 attraction] alteration *O, cor. M*. 38 Cursings threatning damnation or]
cursing damnation to *O*; thretténing *inserted in M*. 39 barraine] forraine *O*.
faults] factes *E*. 40 Collusion] conclusion *O, cor. M*.

PAGE 28

1 We remitt] I omit *E, O*. 4 and Maiestie] *om. O*. 6 report] refer *M*.
8 not] *deleted M*. 11 expected] exacted *E, O*. Loanes, men] Leuies, Men
E; Persons *O, cor. M*. 12 their goods] our Goods *O, cor. M*. 14 of so
weake] so weake of *E*. 16 This the world] This world *O, cor. M*.
19 any more renowned] any men more renouned *O*. 20 vanity] vaunt *E*.
23 them] their turne *E*. 24 know] be knowen *O, cor. M*. 27 indignity]
indignation *O, cor. M*. 28 Queene] Noble Queene *O*. 30 impossible]
most vaine, and so impossible *O*. 33 infinite seers and hearers, deliuer] so
many and so infinite people, as well seers as hearers, euen *O*. 35 is in]
is so often, and in *O*. 36 Confesse] confesse manifestly *O*. 40 1500.]
xvᶜ hundred *E*.

PAGE 29

6 vertue and doctrine god] Doctrine and vertue God Almightie *O*.
7 Damianus] *so O*; Danuanus *A*; Dimianus *E*. **8** into our Cuntry] *om. O*.
9 Lucius] Lucas *E*. **10** Company] companions *O*. **11** all within] who
in *O*, *cor. M*. within...were all] *om. E*. **12** derived] deuided *O*, *cor. M*.
13 Eleutherius] Clutherinus *E*. **18** favourers] *so E, O*; favours *A*. **20** soe]
om. O, added M. **23** excellency] exellency *A*. **24** Reliques] relictes *E*.
25 all] all theyr *O*. **26** owne] *om. O, added M*. **28** finde] see *E*.

PAGE 30

4 Fathers] *so E*; Father *A*, *O*. **9** exempteth] excludeth *O*. **16** nor the
Priesthood in it self] or priesthoode yt selfe *E*, *O*. mynume] minute *E*. **23**
any mites worth] a mite worthy *O*. **24** Lay Catholique] lay-mã *O*. through-
out] through out all *E*; through all *O*. **28** to a] *a added above the line in A*.
29 single] *cor. fr*. vertuous *in A*. **33** Raigne] *inserted above the line in A*.
34 of] *cor. fr*. from *in A*. **37–38** -hood...Priest-] *interlined in A*.

PAGE 31

2 comming in and going out] coming and going *E, O*. **6** attire] attayne *O*.
11 they] that *O, cor. M*. **12** either] neither *O, cor. M*. by] but *O, cor. M*.
by] by any *O, cor. M*. **16** mistitled] *so O*; misliked *A*; distitled *E*. **17** the
basenes of the reproach] base reproach *O, cor. M*. **18** discerning] deseruing *O*. **19** and nothing but Religion] *om. O*. **28** proceeding] Complaine
deleted after this word in A. **29** things] times *E*. **30** besides...partly]
beside our Preisthoode being partly *E*. **34** Arraignement] Arrignement *A*.
35 ample notice; wherin] such an ample notice, as *O*.

PAGE 32

4 obiected somtymes] sometimes obiected *E*; some time obiected *O*. **5**
person] Maiesty *O*. **6** voyd from] wide of *O*. **12** soe savage] sauage and
brutish *O*. **13** Martyrdoms our steppes] Martyrdome, steppes *O*. others]
so E, M; our *A*, *O*. **18** Highnes] Maiesties Highnesse *O*. **26** expected]
suspected *O, cor. M*. **27** meere tolerable] more liberall *E*; more intollerable *O*.
30 Allarme] alarumum *O*, alarum *M*. **32** for] *om. O, inserted M*. **34** feele]
finde *O*. popular] the popular peoples *O*. **35** private] priuie or secret *O*.
37 hope] hope or comfort *O*. **39** heavier] hevier *A*.

PAGE 33

1 pitty] pietie *O*. **3** quartane] quarrell *E*. **5** mens more] men, more *O*.
7 weak] weake and tender *O*. enemies] manie enimies *O*. **8** battered]
battered and beaten *O*. be both dangerous] be amongst manie accounted
most daungerous *O*. **14** our] your *O, cor. M*. **15** violence] violente *O*,
cor. M. **18** lowliest] lowest *O, cor. M*. **23** pressed] proceeded *O*. **24** of
torture] or torment *E*. **27** of Contempt] for Contempt *E*; for euerie one *O*.
30 tortures] torments *O*. reveale] reuile *O, cor. M*. **33** Interrogatories]
interogations *O*. **34** our action...those] *om. E*. whom] which *E*. **36** were]
are *O, cor. M*. **39** panges] paines *E*.

PAGE 34

8 tyring] trying *O, cor. M.*   **9** damning] dammaging *E.*   **10** satisfie] suffice *O, cor. M.*   **13** tortures] tormentes *O.*   **14** booted and Cloathed] bobed & clogged *O, cor. M.*   **16** Some haue bene watched] *om. O.*   **25** very] *so E, O; om. A.*   **37** are we forced] we are most cruelly enforced *O.*   **38** a felicity] their onely felicitie *O.*   **39** their] their greedye *O.*

PAGE 35

14 fight] not take part *O.*   **15** his] *so E, O;* in *A.*   **17** duties] deathes *O.*   **31** Cuntrie] enimies *O.* Cuntries] cuntrey *E, O.*   **32** Confession] confusion *O.*   **34** the Pope] be Pope *O.*

PAGE 36

5 of those that goe over] *so E, O; om. A.*   **8** follies] fables *E.* which hearing] which all protestântes hearing *O.*   **9** Potentates] protestants *O.* to their face] *om. O.*   **10** small] *om. O.*   **17** know to be but a bundell] knewe to be a kinde *O.*   **20** now trust more vpon] then trust to *O.*   **21** our] *cor. fr.* his in *A.*   **22** increasing his] encreaseth his more *O.*   **26** wisdome shew scrowles of] wise deliuer *E.*   **30** be so vnwise as to] but *O.*   **33** of Spaine] *om. E, O.*   **38** Intelligence] intelligences *E;* intelligencers *O.*   **39** States] *so E, O;* Estates *A.* Invasion] innovation *E.*

PAGE 37

3 vnproved] vnprouided *O.*

PAGE 38

15 more] more | more *A.*   **19** professed and] *om. E;* enemies *deleted after* professed in *A.*   **22** Adalantado...Spaine] Spanish Captaines *E.*   **24** their] *cor. fr.* his in *A; om. E.*   **26** Captiues] Captaines *E, O.*   **34** are] *cor. fr.* as in *A.*   **39** Confitents] conficent *O.*

PAGE 39

5 readily] readie *O.*   **6** mayne] many *E, O.*   **10** and daily] *om. O.*   **11** Indies] Indians *E.*   **12** since] even since *E, O.*   **13** beggered] *cor. fr.* beggerly in *A;* beggerlie *O.*   **16** vntruth] truth *E;* vntruthes *O.*   **24** now to] knowne to the *O.*   **32** soone be taken, that] seene some token *E.*

PAGE 40

1 Wisbiche] *om. E, O.*   **3** incommodities] commodities *O.*   **5** in durance] *so E;* endurance *A, O.* Religion] recusancye *E.*   **6** Church, pine] Church. Pining *O.*   **13** the few] those few *E;* these *O.*   **15** spirituall] speciall *O.*   **23** posterities] *so E, O;* prosperities *A.*   **24** we are] *cor. fr.* are we in *A.* iniured] incurred *O.*   **26** railing] *added above the line in A.*   **34** to be popular] for to popular *E;* to be too popular *O.*

PAGE 41

1 stile] Testament *O.*   **6** committed] committed to prison *O.*   **12** were] *cor. fr.* we say in *A.*   **13** occasioners] occasions *E.*   **14** but issue] *cor. fr.* issue but in *A.* vnearned] *cor. fr.* vniformed in *A;* vndeserued *E;* vniformed *O.*   **33** Corrasiues] corrisiues *O.*   **35** for redresse] to haue redresse *E, O.*

PAGE 42

4 doing vs] *cor. fr.* deeming our *in A*; deeming our *E*. **14** profession] confession *O*. Faith] speech *O*. **15** presence] present *O*. **17** before men] *om. O*. men,...him before] *om. E*. **19** better] greater *E*. **21** by their most] then most *O*. **25** presence] presents *O*.

PAGE 43

7 Leases] *cor. in margin fr.* Law *in A*; leases of recusants lands *E*; leases of Protestants hands *O*. **10** violently] seuerely *O*. where] whereas *E, O*. **18** vsage] abuses, *E, O*. **20** commended] coũitted *deleted before this word in A*. **23** other] to their *E*. **24** soe] see *O*. **31** fortunes] foũtains *O*. **35** can...eares] *om. E*.

PAGE 44

2 their] *so E, O*; our *A*. **3** offspring] offpp *deleted before this word in A*. **7** sealed] seasoned *O*. **14** open all] openly *O*. **17** lotts] blotts *E, O*. **19** dispatching] displacing *E*; displeasing *O*. **22** sure of many that] sure that many *E, O*. **23** heave his] haue the *O*. **24** Parents] father *E, O*. **35** Continuance] Cruel *deleted before this word in A*.

PAGE 45

7 of sorrowes...grow] *om. E*. **10** continued] Continuall *E*. **11** sparkle] sparke *O*. **14** soe farr of from] too farre for *O*. **18** ayme] out *E*. **21** them] vnto you *deleted after this word in A*. **32** lenitiue] *so E*; lenity *A, O*. **33** time] season *E*. **34** enforced] forced *E, O*. **35** extracted] extorted *O*. **37** implying] imploying *O*. Highnes] Maiesties *O*.

PAGE 46

1 intended] *om. E*. **2** humble] *om. E*. **3** sureties] faithes *E, O*. **5** you] your Highnes *E*. **6** Comfort] Comfortes *E*. **7** This last of December] December 31. A°. 1592 *E*; December 14. Anno. 1595. *O*.

APPENDIX I

THE PROCLAMATION OF 1591

[*S.T.C.* 8207. From the copy in the Folger Shakespeare Library]

❧ By the Queene

A declaration of great troubles pretended against the Realme by a number of Seminarie Priests and Iesuists, sent, and very secretly dispersed in the same, to worke great Treasons vnder a false pretence of Religion, with a prouision very necessary for remedy thereof. Published by this her Maiesties Proclamation.

Although we haue had probable cause to haue thought, that now towards the end of xxxiii. yeres, being the time wherein almightie God, hath continually preserued vs in a peaceable possession of our kingdoms, the former violence & rigor of the malice of our enemies (specially of the King of Spaine) would after his continuance in seeking to trouble our state, without any iust cause so many yeeres, haue waxed faint and decayed in him, and all others depending on him, and bene altered into some peaceable humour, meete to haue disposed him to liue in concord with vs, and other Christian Princes his neighbours, and by such good meanes to establish an vniuersall peace in Christendome now by his warres onely, and no otherwise disturbed: yet to the contrary we find it, by his present mighty actions, so great as he neuer before this time attempted the like. Whereby it so pleaseth the Almightie God of Hostes, (as we are perswaded) to suffer the ruine or correction of such as will not be content to liue in peace with their owne: And to that ende, to permit the said king now in this his declined yeeres meetest for peace, and when he ought to be satisfied, without seeking of more kingdomes, by violence and armes (seeing hee possesseth at this day, more Crownes, Kingdomes and Countries, and more earthly wealth then any of his progenitours, or any other Prince Christian euer had) now to beginne a most uniust and a dangerous warre for all Christendome against the present French King. As in like maner appeared he meant two yeeres past to haue done the like against vs, by inuading of our kingdomes, in the verie time of a treatie of peace with vs. Whereof God gaue him and his whole army a iust cause of repentance.

1 And therefore seeing we do now manifestly vnderstand, that he hath of late (to fortifie these his strange violent attempts with some newe coulour) procured a *Milanois* a vassaile of his owne to be exalted into the Papacie of Rome, and hath seduced him, without consent of the College of Cardinalles to exhaust the treasures of the Church, and therewith to leuie forces in Italie (which had no sound of warre in it these many yeeres) and in many other places, to be guyded by his Nephew, and sent to inuade France, a kingdome that hath bene alwayes a maintainer of that Church in al their oppressions. And for that this warre, so generally, and mightily against France, concerneth our estate very greatly, & can not but be directly very dangerous to our dominions: And that it is also knowen to vs, that by sundry means, besides the preparation of other great forces for the seas, against our Crowne & Dominions, the same be greater for this yere to come, then euer he had before. And for furtherance therof, hath also lately by color of this his peculiar Popes authority, which he hath nowe hanging at his girdle, practised with certaine principall seditious heads, being vnnatural subiects of our kingdom (but yet very base of birth) to gather together with great labors vpon his charges, a multitude of dissolute yong men, who haue partly for lacke of liuing, partly for crimes committed, become Fugitiues, Rebelles, and Traitors, and for whom there are in Rome, and Spaine, and other places certaine receptacles made to liue in, and there to be instructed in Schoole pointes of sedition, and from thence to be secretly and by stealth conueyed into our Dominions, with ample authoritie from Rome, to mooue, stirre vp, and perswade as many of our subiects, as they dare deale withall, to renounce their naturall allegeance due to vs and our Crowne, and vpon hope by a Spanish Inuasion to be enriched and endowed with the possessions and dignities of our other good subiects: For which purpose they doe binde our subiects (with whom they practise) by Othes, yea by Sacraments to forsweare their naturall alleageance to vs, and yeelde their obedience with all their powers to this King of Spaine and to assist his forces. And for the more forcible attraction of these vnnaturall people, (being weake of vnderstanding) to this their bend, these Seedmen of treason bring certaine Buls from the Pope, some of Indulgences pretending to promise heauen to such as wil yeelde, and some of cursings, threatning damnation and hell, to such as shall not yeelde to their perswasions: And though these maner of Popish attempts, haue bene of long time vsed, yet in some sort also they

haue bene impeached, by direct execution of lawes against such traitors for meere treasons, and not for any poynts of religion, as their fautours would colour falsely their actions, which are most manifestly seene and heard at their arraignements how they are neither executed, cõdemned, nor endited, but for high treasons, affirming amongst other things, that they will take part with any army sent by the Pope against vs & our Realme. And of this that none do suffer death for matter of religion, there is manifest proofe in that a number of men of wealth in our realme professing contrary religiõ, are knowen not to be impeached for the same, either in their liues, landes, or goodes, or in their liberties, but onely by payment of a pecuniary summe, as a penalty for the time that they do refuse to come to Church, which is a most manifest course to falsifie the slanderous speeches and Libelles of the Fugitiues abroade. Yet now it is certainely vnderstoode, that these heads of these dennes & receptacles, which are by the traitours called Seminaries, and Colleges of Iesuits, haue very lately assured the King of Spaine, that though heretofore he had no good successe with his great forces, against our Realme, yet if now he will once againe renewe his warre this next yeere, there shall be found ready secretely within our Dominions, many thousands (as they make their accompt for their purpose) of able people that will be ready to assist such power as he shall set on land, and by their vaine vaunting, they do tempt the King hereto, who otherwise ought in wisdome, & by his late experience conceiue no hope of any safe landing here: shewing to him in Spaine, by the special information of a Scholeman named *Parsons*, arrogating to himselfe the name of the King Catholikes Confessour, and to the Pope at Rome, by an other Scholler called *Allen*, now for his treasons, honoured with a Cardinalles Hatte, certaine skrolles or beadrolles of names, of men dwelling in sundry partes of our Countries, as they haue imagined them, but specially in the maritimes, with assurance, that these their Seedmen named Seminaries, Priests, & Jesuites are in the sundry parts of the Realme secretly harbored, hauing a great part of them bene sent within these x. or xii. moneths, and shall be ready to continue their reconciled people in their lewde constancie to serue their purpose both with their forces, and with other trayterous enterprises when the Spanish power shall be ready to land, vpon which their impudent assertions to the Pope, and to the King of Spaine (though they knowe a great part thereof to be false) they haue now very lately aduertised into diuers partes by their secret messengers, whereof some are also very lately taken, and haue confessed the same, that the King vpon their informations and requestes hath promised to imploy all his forces that he can, by sea this next yere, to attempt once again the inuasion of this realme: Wherewith because some of his wisest counsellers doubt that he shall not preuaile, therefore hee is otherwise perswaded, that if that his purpose shall not take place here, yet the same may be well imployed against France or the Lowe Countries, or against some part of Scotland, into which Realme there hath also some number of the like brood bene lately sent.

2 Wherefore considering that these the intentions of the King of Spaine, are to vs in this sort made very manifest, And although we doubt not, but almightie God, the defender of all iust causes, will (as alway hitherto he hath) make the same voyde: Yet it is our dutie as being the supreme Gouernor vnder his Almightie hand, to vse al such iust & reasonable meanes as are giuen to vs, and therewith to concurre or rather attend vpon his most gracious fauour by the helpe of our faithfull subiects, both to encrease our forces to the vttermost of their powers, and by execution of Lawes, and by all other politike ordinances to impeach the foresayd practises of these seditions and treasons.

3 And before al other things, we do first require of the Ecclesiastical state, that the like diligence be vsed by the godly Ministers of the Church, by their diligent teaching & example of life, to retaine our people stedfastly in the profession of the Gospell, and in their duties to almightie God and vs, as it is seene a fewe Capitall heads of treasons are continually occupied with their Seminaries, in withdrawing of a multitude of ignorants to their enchantments.

4 And secondly, for hauing of sufficient forces in readinesse by Sea, we hope by Gods goodnesse, and with the help of our good Subiects, to haue as great, or greater strength on the Seas then at any time we haue had, to withstand these puffed vaunts from Spaine: And for our forces by land, our trust is, that seeing we haue distributed our whole realme into seuerall charges of Lieutenancies, that they by themselues where they may be personally present, & otherwise by their Deputies, & assistants of other our Ministers, will now after the generall Musters which haue bene by our special order lately taken, consider of all things requisite to performe, and make perfect all defects that shall appeare necessarie, to make all the bands both of horsemen and footemen fully furnished with armour,

weapons, and munition, and with all other things requisite for their conduction to the places of seruice, and there also to continue as time shall require to defende their Countrey. And so we doe most earnestly require and charge all maner of our Subiects, with their handes, purses, and aduises, yea all and euery person of euery estate, with their prayers to God, to moue him to assist this so naturall, honorable, and profitable a seruice being only for defence of their naturall Countrey, their wiues, families, children, lands, goods, liberties, and their posterities against rauening strangers, wilfull destroyers of their Natiue countrey and monstrous traytours.

5   And lastly, to withstand & prouide speedy remedy against the other fraudulent attempts of the Seminaries, Iesuites, and Traitors, without the which (as it appeareth) the forces should not be nowe vsed, the same being wrought onely by falsehoode, by hypocrisie, and by vnderminings of our good Subiects vnder a false colour and face of holines, to make breaches in mens and womens consciences, and so to traine them to their Treasons and that with such a secrecie by the harboring of the sayd traiterous messengers in obscure places, as without very diligent and continuall search to be made, and seuere orders executed, the same will remaine and spred it selfe as a secret infection of treasons in the bowels of our Realme, most dangerous, yea, most reprochfull to be suffered in any well ordered common weale: Therefore we haue determined by aduise of our Counsell, to haue speedily certaine Commissioners, men of honesty, fidelitie, and good reputation to be appointed in euery Shire, Citie, and Port townes within our Realme, to enquire by all good meanes what persons are by their behauiours or otherwise worthy to be suspected to be any such persons, as haue bene sent, or that are imployed in any such perswading of our people or of any residing within our Realme to treason, or to moue any to relinquish their allegeance to vs, or to acknowledge any kinde of obedience to the Pope, or to the King of Spaine, and also of all other persons that haue bene thereto induced, and that haue thereto yeelded, And further to proceede in the execution of such their Commission as they shall be more particularly directed by instructions annexed to their sayd Commission.

6   And furthermore, because it is certainely knowen & proued by common experience, vpon the apprehension of sundry of the sayde trayterous persons sent into the Realme, that they doe come into the same by secret Creekes, and landing places, disguised, both

in their names and persons. Some in apparell, as Souldiers, Mariners, or Merchants, pretending that they haue bene heretofore taken prisoners, and put into Gallies, and deliuered. Some come in as gentlemen with contrary names, in comely apparell, as though they had trauailed into Forreine countreys for knowledge: And so generally all, or the most part, as soone as they are crept in, are cloathed like gentlemen in apparel, and many as gallants, yea in all colours, and with feathers, and such like disguising themselues, and many of them in their behauior as Ruffians, farre off to be thought, or suspected to be Friers, Priests, Iesuits, or Popish schollers. And of these many doe attempt to resort into the Vniuersities and houses of Law from whence in former times they departed: many into seruices of Noble men, Ladies and gentlemen, with such like fraudulent deuises to couer themselues from all apprehension, or suspicion: and yet in processe of time, they do at length so insinuate themselues to get themselues credite with hypocrisies, as they infect both the Masters and Families, and consequently aduenture also yea secretly to vse their offices of priesthood and reconcilements: Whereby al such as do retayne them are worthie to be suspected, and may be charged by law to their great danger.

7 For auoyding wherof, and either to discouer these venemous vipers, or to chase them away out of the Realme from the infecting of many more, We do order and straightly charge and command all maner of persons of what degree soeuer they be without any exception, Spirituall, or Temporall, Nobelman, Gentleman, Lord, Lady, Master or Mistresse, or owner whatsoeuer of any house, familie, lodging, yea the verie Officers of our owne houshold, and Gouernours of any societies, to make a present due and particular Inquisition of all maner of persons that haue bene admitted, or suffered to haue vsual resort, diet, lodging, residence in their houses, or in any place by their appointment, at any time within the space of one whole yeere now past, and ended at Michaelmas last: Or that from thenceforth haue, or shalbe admitted, or suffered so to resort, eate, lodge, reside or attend: And by such Inquisition and examination, to be duely and particularly informed of what condition and countrie any such person is, and by what kind of meanes he hath heretofore liued, and where he hath spent his time for the space of one whole yere before. And likewise to know whether he hath vsed, & doth vse to repaire to the Church at vsuall times to diuine seruice, according to the lawes of the Realme. And to cause those Inquisi-

tions, with their answeres to be put into writing particularly, and the same to keepe in a maner of a Register or Kalender to be shewed when they shalbe demanded, that vpon cause of suspition of any such person, the same may be further tried by the Commissioners of those places, whether the same persons so examined be loyal subiects or no. And if any such shalbe found vnwilling to answere to such Inquisition, or shall be found by his doubtfull answere not likely to be an obedient subiect, the same person shall bee stayd by the housholder, or him that ought to haue examined him and shall be sent to any of the Commissioners aboue mentioned next adioyning. And if any person hauing gouernment or commandement ouer any such seruant, or resiant, shall be found not to haue performed the points of the foresaid Inquisition as is aboue limitted, the same shall bee called to appeare before the sayd Commissioners, or before our priuie Counsell, if the qualitie of the person shall so require, and shall bee further vsed and ordered for such default, as the said Commissioners, or our Counsel shal haue iust cause to deale with such a person. And finally, we doe admonish and straitly charge and command all persons that haue had any intelligence, with any such so sent or come from beyond the seas to such purposes, to detect them to the Commissioners in that behalfe to bee assigned as aforesayd, within xx. dayes after the publication hereof, in the Shire, Towne, or Citie, or Port, within the precincts of the same Commission, vpon payne that the offenders therein, shalbe punished as abettors & mainteiners of traytors. Wherein we are resolutely determined to suffer no fauor to be vsed for any respect of any persons, qualities, or degrees, nor shal allow, or suffer to be allowed any excuse of negligence for not detection, or for not due examination of the qualities of such dangerous persons according to the order hereafore prescribed, being no wise contrary, but agreeable to the most ancient lawes and good vsages of our Realme, deuised for the good order of all maner of Subiects in euery precinct of any Leete to be forthcomming to answere for their behauior towards the dignitie of our Crowne, and the common peace of our Realme. Giuen at our Mannor of Richmond the xviii. of October, *1591*, in this xxxiii. yeere of our raigne.

God saue the Queene.

❧ Imprinted at London by the Deputies of Christopher Barker, Printer *to the Queenes most excellent Maiestie.*

APPENDIX II

THE PROCEEDINGS IN ROME IN 1602

(*a*)

[From *The Archpriest Controversy*, ed. T. G. Law
(Camden Society, 1898), II, 95–98.]

Ex Supplicatione Patris Roberti Suthvvelli Jesuitæ ad Reginam Angliæ anno Dñi 1595 impressa, et publicata Jesuitis in Anglia post eius mortem, cuius nomen licet non sit affixum patet tamen ex stilo et manuscripto de quo diù mirifice gloriabantur Jesuitæ, ex fama publica et testibus in Anglia fide dignissimis, ab eo fuisse confectum et ex confessione impressoris qui eam ob causam suspendio fuit affixus, à Jesuitis fuisse impressum; verum ne in eos odium nominatim deriuetur satis erit ad Scandala tollenda, quæ Catholicis ex hac impressione sunt exorta, librum ipsum sine authore condemnare.

Fol. 73 [39].[1] Satis justam belli causam dicit fuisse Regi Catolico inuadendi Angliam quod inter cetera opem tulerunt Regi Christianissimo, id temporis inimico Hispaniæ contra jus et titulum Infantæ, filiæ Regis Catolici quod habuit in Britanniam; quod ualde iniuriosum uidetur Regi Christianissimo et Coronæ Franciæ.

Fol. eodem. Neque leuis est iniuria illata Celsitudini tuæ, cum sacratam illam manum tuam a talibus cogitationibus directam quæ dedignantur falsitates patronas habere vestrarum actionum uideri uelint authorem huius sententiæ.

Fol. 84 [44]. Reginam excusat tanquam persecutionis insciam, et leuissimam, tenerrimam, et inimicam crudelitatis.

Fol. 86 [45]. Quod nunquam procedere posse speramus à tam molli et gratioso Judice, sicut est sacrata sua persona, aut sicut es tu ipsa sacrata ibidem; quod est magis incidens in illam mitissimam temperiem excellentissimi animi sui.

Fol. eodem [46]. Accipe igitur (Princeps clementissima) et consule in bonam partem omnia humillima obsequia, et fidelitates nostras quæ cum cogitationibus fidissimis, et resolutionibus seruicij plenis sunt sine aliqua simulatione desponsata in maiestatis vestræ defensionem.

Fol. 70 [36–37]. Tanquam honoris causa notat P. Personium et

---

[1] Figures in square brackets refer to the pages in the present edition.

laudat, quod non sit nouitius in scientia secretorum et intelligentiarum Principum, quod tamen ipse libenter non confitetur.

Fol. 88[1] [35–36]. Laudi dat P. Personio quod sit Veteranus in rebus politicis.

Fol. 61 [32–33]. Reginam mira adulatione excusat tanquam à persecutione abhorrentem.

Fol. 56 [30]. Virtutem Reginæ in uita illa quam sibi elegit celibi et innupta laudat.

Fol. 56 [30]. Dicit Papam in sacerdotibus initiandis nec sibi uindicare nec acquirere maiorem in Anglia auctoritatem quam qui Basiliæ aut Geneuæ sunt Pseudoministri in creandis ministris protestantibus.

Fol. 46 [25]. Vestra Regalis maiestas semper subijciendo desideria sua virtutis normæ et regalitatem suam moderando magis uoluntate ignoscendi quam potestate interficiendi nunquam consensum prebuit tam uilibus et horrendis imposturis.

Pag^a 1ma [1]. Potentissima, misericordiosissima maximèque amanda et timenda Princeps.

2 [1]. Bonitas maiestatis vestræ perfecta in omnibus officijs Principe dignis, solaque nostræ iustæ spei anchora sacra.

27 [14]. Quem ad finem persuaderemus Catholicis, ut vestræ ma^{ti} debitam obijciant obedientiam; quando nec nobis nec ipsis hoc prodesse queat.

28 [16]. Si incorrupta ratio judex constituatur, nunquam pronunciabit infidelitatem sequi posse, ex quocunque nostræ Religionis articulo, quæ sanè religio nos magis astringit quam alios quoscunque ad exactissimam submissionem prestandum Vestræ temporali auctoritati, ad eaque omnia honoris ac fidelitatis obsequia quæ Catholici populi aut nostris suæ aut anteactis temporibus cuiquam Principi Christiano debita agnouerunt et detulerunt.

42 [23–24]. Si illi consiliarium quem, imo si V. M^{tem} sacram, à Regno sustulissent (id quod Dei bonitas hactenus nec permisit nec, ut sperare licet, inposterum permittet) consilia tamen sua ne speciem quidem optati exitus habuissent.

34^2 [28]. Sacrum nomen nostræ nobilissimæ Reginæ tale est, ut proximè post dei uerbum inter firmissima ueritatis testimonia honorandum sit.

59 [32]. Obiectum aliquando sacerdotibus fuit, quasi de uita sacræ maiestatis vestræ aliquid moliti essent, quæ res est adeo

---

[1] P. 68 is misnumbered 88 in the octavo edition. [2] An error for 52.

institutis eorum contraria, atque à cogitationibus suis publicaque utilitate aliena, ut qui rationem in consilium adhibebit, is nulla ratione existimabit sacerdotes tam stultos, ut rem non modo tam inutilem prorsus sed etiam penitus odiosam uel cogitarent, multo minus perficerent.

60 [32]. Nemini obscurum esse potest quam pernitiosum futurum sit sacerdotibus ac Catholicis vestræ maiestatis protectione destitui.

60 [32]. Mors maiestatis vestræ infinitam perturbationem rerum inferret maioremque omnibus calamitatem quam Catholicis consolationis causam, ut nos sacerdotes illam machinari esset non solum impium in patriam, sed etiam in nosmetipsos iniuriosum.

62 [33]. Malumus nos vestræ confidere clementiæ, ijsque fauoribus et gratijs quas M^{tas} Vestra secundum Deum nobis facere maximas potest, quàm in humana quadam in Dei unctos uiolentia pestem patriæ et nobismetipsis incommodum illud quo nihil grauius importare.

62 [33]. Quatenus vero obijcitur aliquos nostrum affirmasse: uelle se Papæ exercitus partes tueri contra nostrum Regnum; est sane nullo modo uerisimile nisi ex fragili lingua tormentorum ui prodijsset.

67 [35]. Hoc vestræ maiestati firmissimè asseueramus quisquis ille fuerit, uel cuiusque generis exercitus qui contra te uenerit, potius pectora nostra inimicorum gladijs transfodienda obijciemus, quam gladios nostros in patrij sanguinis effusionem conuertemus. Haec, et similia habet ista supplicatio pag. 23. 30. 26. 66. [13, 16, 14, 35] et alibi. Neque male affectus animus, neque ueritas, sed tortura sola linguam direxit quæ locuta est talia procul dubio fuerunt uerba illa allegata de tuendis partibus exercitus Papæ contra nostrum Regnum si unquam de ore sacerdotis prodierunt aut alitèr ab aliquo imperito laico fuerunt dicta. pag. 66. [35] unde concludit non esse ueram illam propositionem debere sacerdotem Cath. tueri partes exercitus Pontificij contra hereticos.

(b)

'Memorial presented by the agents of the Archpriest not to allow the *Supplication*, against which the Appellants were objecting, to be condemned, as their text may have been depraved.'

[From the transcript from Stonyhurst MS. P. 466 among Fr. J. H. Pollen's *Southwell Scripta* at the Farm Street House.]

Beatissime Pater. Intelligimus delatum nuper ad S.V. libellum quendam supplicium qui ad reginam Angliae praeteritis annis in favorem quorundam nobilium catholicorum a religioso quodam viro fuerat exhibitus; qua certe re non leviter commoti sumus, atque officii nostri esse duximus S. Vᵃ. fideliter paucisque referre quae tam de ipso libro quam de ejus authore nos esse verissima scimus. Et quidem author ejusmodi supplicis libelli noscitur fuisse P. Rob. Southwellus Soc. J. presbyter nobilis apud nostrates familiae vir doctus ac pius qui alios etiam edidit libros eruditissimos ac rei Catholicae utilissimos ac post in Anglicana messe labores ac deinde carceres ac saepius repetita tormenta constantissime pro tuenda fide ac sede Apostolica martyrium passus est ad annum D. 1595. Porro libellus iste supplex scriptus ac reginae oblatus est anno D. 1587, quem nos manuscriptum legimus, neque enim unquam ab authore typis est mandatus, nihilque nisi pium tantoque viro dignum in illo deprehendimus: quod si verbis blandioribus atque honorificis reginam quandoque compellet, ut inde Catholicis valde per id tempus afflictis levamen aliquod procuraret, certe hoc et res ipsa, postulavit habuitque aliorum virorum gravium et Card^{lis} Alani hac in parte examplum quod sequeretur; et quod caput est hoc ipsum fuerat a fel. rec. Gregorio XIII Patribus Societatis in Angliam Anno D. 1580 proficiscentibus praescriptum, ut in rebus omnibus ad statum civilem pertinentibus pro legitima eam regina haberent, atque externo honore verbisque observarent, quoad Sedes Apostolica aliud hac in parte statueret. Quodsi v° quippiam his liber nunc impressus in rebus fidei minus consulte scriptum complecti inveniretur, illud S^{ti} V^{ae} sincere sancteque profitemur arbitrari nos id omne spurium atque suppositum esse, a quopiam qui post martyris obitum (quo anno atque intentione Deus novit) libellum hunc praelo dandum curavit, additum atque adsutum. Quare a S. Vestra omni qua possumus contentione supplices petimus, ne pati velit indignissimam hanc notam illius viri nomini ac memoriae inuri, qui pro fide Catholica atque hac sta. Sede vitam ipsam et sanguinem profudit. Supplicamus etiam ut ipsiusmet libelli nobis copia fiat, et ut nobis liceat objecta omnia contra martyrem sigillatum repellere atque diluere. &c.

APPENDIX III

DONNE AND SOUTHWELL

In the third chapter of his *Pseudo-Martyr* (1610) Donne singles out several 'erroneous doctrines' of the Roman Church, of which the first is its practice of 'abasing, and auiling the Dignitie and persons of secular Magistrates, by extolling Ecclesiasticke immunities and priuiledges'. From this topic he passes to a discussion of the extravagance of certain royal and ecclesiastical titles, from which he concludes that

the farthest mischief, which by this excesse Princes could stray into, or subiects suffer, is a deuiation into Tyranny, and an ordinary vse of an extraordinary power and prerogatiue....But by the magnifying of the Bishoppe of Rome with these Titles, our religion degenerates into superstition; which is a worse danger.[1]

Two more pages of citation and argument, levelled mainly against the Jesuit writers on the subject, end with a fling at the 'iniquitie and peruersenesse of those men, who thinke great Titles belong to Kings, not as Kings, but as Papisticall Kings;' and then follows this paragraph:

For so at a Consultation of *Iesuites* in the *Tower* in the late Queenes time, I saw it resolued, that in a Petition to bee exhibited to her, shee might not be stiled *Sacred*. Though one of their owne Order[2] haue obserued that attribute to bee so cheape, that it was vsuall to say, *Sancti Patres conscripti*, and *Sacratissimi Quirites*, and *Sanctissimi Milites*. And our English *Iesuites* vse to aggrauate her defection much, by that circumstance, that shee had been Consecrated, and pontifically Anoynted, and inuested at her Coronation, and therefore was Sacred.[3]

'Sacer' or 'sacred' was still common in royal titles of the sixteenth and seventeenth centuries. For instance, in the dedicatory epistle to *Pseudo-Martyr* Donne saluted James I as 'Most mightie and sacred Soueraigne', and James himself addressed his *Premonition* to 'the most sacred and invincible Prince, Rodolphe the II. by Gods clemencie elect Emperour of the Romans'. Nevertheless, to interpret 'sacred' here as meaning consecrated was mere rationalization,

[1] P. 43.
[2] A marginal note gives a reference to Serarius, *Litaneutic.* l. 2 q. 4 n. 4.
[3] P. 46.

since such titles were ultimately derived from those of the ancient Roman emperors and their claims to divinity.

But the important sentence in Donne's paragraph is the first one. In it he affirms that the English Jesuits had refused to allow Elizabeth to be addressed as sacred—which is scarcely as surprising as that they, the most determined and implacable of her Catholic opponents, should ever have been parties to a petition addressed to her. The wording of the petition had been formally discussed at a gathering held—of all places !—in the Tower of London; and Donne had been present. The problem is to decide whether this incident could have had any relation to Southwell's *Supplication*.

In attempting to determine with any certainty the time-limits within which the event mentioned by Donne might have occurred it is difficult to be precise. The *terminus a quo* should be as early as possible; no more is necessary than that Donne should have been old enough to be admitted to such a gathering. As for the *terminus ad quem*, the earliest specific statements from Donne himself that he was a Protestant are to be found in two letters written to Sir George More on 11 and 13 February 1601/2, shortly after his marriage, but it is probable that he had ceased to regard himself as a Catholic some years previously. Walton pictures him as assailed by doubts during his Lincoln's Inn days;[1] he 'did...presently lay aside all study of the law...and began seriously to survey and consider the body of divinity as it was then controverted betwixt the Reformed and the Roman Church'. About a year later he 'did show the then Dean of Gloucester...all [Bellarmine's] works marked with many weighty observations under his own hand'—a sign at least that he was seriously discussing matters of faith with Protestant divines. His indecision may have persisted until early in 1596, when the *Third Satire* was probably written; during the next two years the expeditions of 1596 and 1597 not only involved him in lengthy absences from England but to some extent diverted his mind elsewhere. One may reasonably conjecture that when he entered Egerton's service at the end of 1597 his mind was made up and he had decided to throw in his lot on the side of Protestant orthodoxy. The incident referred to in *Pseudo-Martyr* therefore occurred before 1602 and most probably before 1596.

[1] Walton's chronology here is not strictly accurate; he says that Donne entered Lincoln's Inn at seventeen (in reality he was twenty) and speaks of him as being 'unresolved in his religion' in 'the nineteenth year of his age'.

Catholic petitions to the sovereign were not encouraged during the last twenty years of Elizabeth's reign. Richard Shelley, who put one into her hand in March 1585 'at such time as she walked in her parke at Greenewitch', was promptly thrown into prison by Walsingham and left to die there. Though his nominal offence was merely that he had presented his petition directly to the Queen and not through the intermediary of the Council, his example served as a salutory warning to others.

Of the three petitions known to have been presented to Elizabeth by the Catholics between 1583 and her death, the last can, for present purposes, be fairly easily eliminated. It came from the appellant party, and reached the Queen, through the connivance of Bishop Bancroft, in the summer of 1601. Elizabeth read it carefully in the presence of her Council, and rejected it with the comment: 'The King of France, truly, may without peril of honour, life, or kingdom, grant liberty of religion, but it is not so with me, for if I grant this liberty to Catholics, by this very fact I lay at their feet myself, my honour, my crown, and my life.' But at this late date Donne was almost certainly no longer a Catholic, and was thus unlikely to be admitted to Catholic counsels; besides, this petition was drawn up by that group of secular priests who expressly dissociated themselves from the Jesuits, and even asked in it for the suppression of some of their writings.[1]

Of the two earlier petitions Shelley's was the first. In the Parliament which met towards the close of 1584 fresh measures against the Catholics were immediately proposed, and two bills were introduced into the Commons. One was the act which provided that if a recusant failed to pay his fines the Crown might confiscate all his personal property and two-thirds of his real property; the other that all priests ordained since the beginning of the Queen's reign who were found within the kingdom forty days after the act came into force should be judged guilty of treason, and that the harbouring of them should be a felony. These bills were brought into the House of Commons on 19 December, but owing to an adjournment they did not pass both houses until 15 March 1585. They received the royal assent at the close of the session, on 29 March.

Shelley's petition was presented on the day these bills passed both houses. The appeal to the Queen was the last resort; she alone could

[1] See T. G. Law, *A Historical Sketch of the Conflicts between the Jesuits and Seculars*, pp. xcviii–xcic and 156.

now prevent them from becoming law. It is unlikely, however, that Shelley was the author, or sole author, of the petition, as all the accounts speak of it as a petition from the Catholics in general. It is almost certain to have been drawn up and discussed at some private gathering. When it was presented there was but one Jesuit, William Weston, in the whole of England, so it may seem forced to apply Donne's phrase 'a Consultation of *Iesuites*' to the earlier stages of this particular petition. Yet a few weeks previously eleven priests had been in confinement in the Tower, including Donne's uncle Jasper Heywood, superior of the English Jesuits, and James Bosgrave, another member of the order. All these had been dismissed from the Tower on 21 January; with ten other priests they were sentenced to banishment and shipped across to France. The government was unwilling to have them on its hands when the legislation then pending came into force and, with more clemency than it has always been given credit for, got them out of the way. If Shelley's petition were drafted before 21 January, as is not impossible,[1] it might quite conceivably have been the subject of some sort of consultation in the Tower, especially as the rigours of imprisonment were considerably relaxed for the priests after their banishment had been decided on.

We also know that at least one member of Donne's immediate family was in touch with the prisoners at this time. William Weston in his autobiography relates the predicament in which he found himself after his arrival in England in September 1584. He was the sole Jesuit in England not in captivity, and he had no means of consulting his superior:

Father Heywood during those days lay detained in captivity within the Tower of London, and besides the other inconveniences of his prison, he was afflicted with divers infirmities. On account of his age and ill health he was permitted to receive visits from his sister, who was able to bestow on him some care and nursing. Through her help, therefore, as she was a Catholic, I transacted some business with him by means of letters, and received letters from him in return. The opening of Parliament was now at hand, that very Parliament in which were decreed those dreadful and ruthless laws against Catholics in general and against the clergy in particular; at which time such priests as were still detained in prison were driven into exile. One of these was Father Heywood, whom I was most intensely

---

[1] Even so, it could not then have received its final form, since it contains a reference to Parry's treason, and Parry was not arrested till 8 February nor executed till 2 March.

anxious to see and converse with before his departure. The matter in consequence being discussed with his sister, and understanding from her that it was possible to bring it to pass without extreme danger, as freer leave of intercourse with his friends would be granted to him in consideration of his removal, I entered with her into the Tower, not without great terror, as I perceived the dreary spaces, the gates and iron bolts past which I was led by my guide, and which enclosed me round. When I came to where the Father was confined, we saluted each other, and then discoursed, as was natural, concerning what we each knew of affairs....

At length, when my conference with Father Heywood was finished, and we had spent almost the whole day together, having embraced him and said a last farewell, I returned by the same labyrinth by which I had entered, and as soon as I found myself outside safe and sound, it seemed as though I was restored to the true light of day.[1]

Weston, writing many years after the event, is not quite certain of his chronology; he says that the meeting of Parliament was 'at hand', then implies that the order for Heywood's banishment was the result of the legislation introduced into Parliament after it met, and finally dates his meeting after Heywood's impending banishment was well known. Nevertheless, it was Donne's mother who conducted him to the Tower, and one has only to suppose that they were accompanied by her thirteen-year-old son to be convinced that this was the occasion recollected years afterwards in *Pseudo-Martyr*. Yet there are several strong objections: (1) At the end of 1584 and the beginning of 1585 Donne is more likely to have been in residence at Oxford, where he had matriculated the previous October, than at home in London; (2) If it was decided that a petition was to be presented to Elizabeth, but that in it she must not be 'stiled Sacred', the fact remains that in the six pages of Shelley's petition she is twice addressed as 'your sacred Maiestie', and there are references as well to her 'sacred blood' and to Parry's 'intended damnable sacrilege';[2] (3) if Heywood, as superior of the Jesuits, had ruled that it was improper to address Elizabeth as 'sacred', it is hard to believe that the word would have been applied to her not only in this document itself, but in another drawn up six years later by another Jesuit.

The third petition to be considered is Southwell's *Supplication*. It is the only document in this form addressed to Elizabeth with

---

[1] John Morris, *The Troubles of our Catholic Forefathers*, 2nd series, pp. 68–69.
[2] There is a copy of Shelley's petition in the Westminster Cathedral Archives, IV, no. 4, fo. 33.

which a Jesuit is known beyond question to have been connected. In it, however, the word 'sacred' is applied to Elizabeth no less than six times.[1] It is interesting to find that five of these six passages were cited by the appellants in their memorial to the Pope, and it is thus quite clear that by 1602 the ruling to which Donne refers was well known to the English Catholics, who also felt quite sure that the word when applied to Elizabeth would be regarded as offensive in Rome. But there is one passage in which the Latin translation does not correspond exactly with the English original. The printed edition (O) of the *Supplication* reads:

your Maiesties goodnesse, (perfect in all Princely duties, & the only shot-anker of our iust hopes),

but the Latin has

Bonitas maiestatis vestræ perfecta in omnibus officijs Principe dignis, solaque nostræ iustæ spei anchora sacra.

It is certain that the appellants had a copy of the printed edition, since they use its text and give page references to it, but it is equally certain that there is no word at this point in the English corresponding to the Latin *sacra*.

One is perhaps scarcely justified in claiming, on the strength of this single example, that Donne's reference must be to Southwell's *Supplication*, but it is difficult to regard the appearance of *sacra* in the Latin translation as a mere accident without any significance. Of course, it is possible that the appellants were merely dishonest in adding the word, but they had plenty of other passages to cite, and their other translations are accurate enough. But, granting that they were not deliberately dishonest and supposing that the *Supplication* was discussed 'at a Consultation of *Iesuites* in the *Tower*', some such hypothesis as the following seems necessary. Southwell probably completed his first draft on 14 December 1591, and made a fair copy which was finished on 31 December, perhaps with the 'Consultation' in view. At the meeting, when the question of the propriety of the word 'sacred' came up, it is likely to have done so in connection with this particular passage, which occurs in the first paragraph and precedes any other uses of the term. One of the appellant priests had also been present at the meeting, and the incident had stuck in his memory, as it had in Donne's, so that he felt justified

[1] See pp. 1, l. 28; 24, l. 1; 28, l. 27; 32, l. 5; 39, l. 15; 45, l. 31.

in inserting the word in the memorial to the Pope in the place where it had once been. After the meeting, one must further suppose, a revised and censored version was prepared for presentation to the Queen, but the copies which got into circulation were all descended from the two earlier versions, from which the objectionable word had been deleted only in the passage to which specific exception had been taken.

If Donne's statement refers to the *Supplication* there are further implications to be faced. It is not easy, for instance, to suggest a satisfactory reason for the choice of so dangerous a meeting-place as the Tower for the discussion of Southwell's petition. There were no Jesuit prisoners to be consulted, and any Jesuits who entered as visitors must have done so with feelings as uncomfortable as those of Weston when he went to visit Heywood. Yet there was one prisoner in 1591 whose influence with Elizabeth had once been considerable, while his rank and lineage gave him an unchallenged place at the head of the Catholic laity. Philip Howard, Earl of Arundel, had been imprisoned in the Tower since 1585. But, though the rigours of his confinement seem to have varied somewhat according to the course of political events, Arundel was a 'close' prisoner; he was not allowed to receive visitors unless they had first secured a warrant from the Council, and then only in the presence of a jailer, and he was allowed out of his quarters only for his daily exercise, during which he was guarded. Nevertheless he was attended by two of his own servants; he wrote and received letters frequently; he could signal to his friends on Tower Hill; and for a time the other Catholic prisoners used to assemble in his quarters to hear mass. There is one further fact of the greatest interest; Southwell lived for several years at Arundel House in the Strand under the protection of the Countess of Arundel, corresponded regularly with the Earl, and acted as the Earl's spiritual adviser until he was himself captured and imprisoned.[1]

Another Catholic prisoner in 1591 was Edmund Neville, claimant to the barony of Latimer, who had also been in the Tower since 1585. He had served in the Spanish armies in the Low Countries, and had been a friend of William Parry. Unlike the Earl of Arundel, he had the liberty of the Tower, and could be visited freely by his friends.

---

[1] The Duke of Norfolk, ed., *The Lives of Philip Howard, Earl of Arundel and Anne Dacres his Wife*, and *The Venerable Philip Howard, Earl of Arundel* (C.R.S., vol. XXI, 1919), pp. 185–90.

Whether the presence of either of these men was sufficient to induce a little group of Catholic visitors, priests and laymen, to enter the Tower to discuss Southwell's *Supplication* it is impossible at this late date to determine. But among them, if visitors there were at the end of 1591 or in the first week or so of 1592, would have been Southwell himself, and doubtless Henry Garnet as the Jesuit superior. Four other Jesuits are known to have been in England at this time, but one would hardly expect all or many of them to have been in London and in the Tower together.

Still another possibility remains to be faced, namely, that Donne was referring to a petition of which no other record has survived. In that case, the intrusive 'sacra' in the appellant memorial would have to be ignored or explained away, and one would be forced to conclude, because of the occurrence of 'sacred' in several other places in Southwell's text, that the episode recalled by Donne happened after, and not before, 1591. But if this was so, the presence of Jesuit prisoners within the Tower between 1591 and 1596 is not of much help in furnishing clues. After the dismissal of Jasper Heywood and his companions the next Jesuit to be confined there was Southwell himself; he was captured on 25 June 1592 and committed to the Tower a few weeks later. He remained there till just before his trial and execution in February 1595. During the last year of his captivity another Jesuit, Henry Walpole, was also in the Tower. They were both 'close' prisoners, and it may be doubted if they were accessible to visitors, since both were subjected to torture.

Long and inconclusive as this discussion has been, it may be said that the balance of probabilities, in the present state of our knowledge, suggests that Donne's reference is to Southwell's *Supplication* rather than to any other known petition, and that if the reference is not to the *Supplication*, it is to an incident after 1591 (but probably not later than 1596)[1] rather than to one before. We can state, then, with some show of likelihood, that at the end of 1591 and perhaps for some time later, Donne was in contact with members of the Jesuit mission in London. Indeed, in view of his mother's connection with earlier members of the mission, first with her brother Jasper Heywood and then with Weston, it is almost inevitable, if he remained a

[1] It may perhaps be added that a petition after about 1592 in which the Jesuits were concerned is rather difficult to conceive, partly because of the effects of Persons's reply to the proclamation, and partly on account of the general hardening of the Jesuit attitude towards Elizabeth.

Catholic, that he should have been. As a result Donne is almost certain to have known Southwell and Garnet, and it is difficult to believe that his relations with them had no effect on his intellectual development.

Donne had entered Thavies Inn by May 1591 and in May 1592 he passed on to Lincoln's Inn. About this time, according to Walton, he plunged into the study of controversial divinity, especially of Bellarmine's works. It has been stated, since Jessopp's time, that Walton is in error in placing Donne's reading of Bellarmine in his nineteenth and twentieth years (1591–92), because the three volumes of *Disputationes de controversiis fidei adversus huius temporis Haereticos* (to which Walton must refer) were not published until 1593. This, however, is not quite accurate. The third volume of Bellarmine's great work, it is true, came out in 1593, but the first volume was published in 1586, and the second in 1588. Donne might therefore have begun to study him in 1591 or earlier, though not necessarily for the purpose suggested by Walton.

The *Disputationes* were based on the lectures which Bellarmine had delivered since 1576 as professor of controversial theology at the Gregorian University in Rome, where it was his function to prepare those in training to become missionary priests in Germany and England:

When Pope Gregory XIII [he wrote] in his zeal to assist Germany and England established two great colleges for the young men of those countries, I was appointed to teach them controversial theology in our schools, and thus, as it were, to arm these new soldiers of the Church for the war with the powers of darkness which they should have to wage when they returned home.[1]

Southwell, Garnet, and Oldcorne were all English members of the Jesuit order who had been his pupils, and were among the first to bring his teachings to England. They must often have cited him; thus it seems likely that through them Donne's attention was first drawn to Bellarmine's writings, so that he became for Donne the leading representative of Jesuit theology.

It is difficult to know what degree of sympathy Donne felt for the Jesuit point of view in 1591 and 1592. The seeds of dissension between Jesuits and seculars in England were already sown, but as yet had

---

[1] Translated and quoted by James Brodrick, *The Life and Work of Blessed Robert Francis Cardinal Bellarmine*, I, 124.

hardly appeared above ground. Still, it is perhaps significant of the fact that Donne's family were no blind adherents of the new generation of Jesuits that a few months after the composition of the *Supplication*, about the very time that Southwell himself was captured, the secular priest William Harrington was captured at Thavies Inn in the rooms of Donne's brother Henry, and Harrington was no friend of the Jesuits. In W. C.'s *Replie unto a certaine Libell* (1603) it is stated that he was so oppressed by Jesuit calumny, that on being offered an opportunity of escape he refused it, saying that 'he must be hanged to prove himself honest'. Nevertheless, at the end of 1591 it was still possible for Southwell in his *Supplication* to speak for all his distressed co-religionists in a way that would have been impossible a short time afterwards. The uncompromising and inflammatory writings of Persons, published between 1592 and 1594, inevitably created a rift among the English Catholics, and from about 1595 onwards the two factions were in open feud. These divisions persisted not only through the whole of the archpriest controversy but continued into the reign of James I and affected the controversy over the oath of allegiance.

Some of the stages of Donne's spiritual pilgrimage can only be surmised, but it seems fair to assume that in 1591 and 1592 he was in sympathy with Southwell's attempt to achieve a reconciliation of Catholicism and patriotism. By the end of his Lincoln's Inn days he had probably reached the sceptical attitude of suspended judgement towards the sects to which the *Third Satire* gave expression, and traces of this attitude persisted until at least 1607, even though, his biographers would have us believe, he was then helping Thomas Morton with his controversial writings on behalf of the Anglican cause.[1] But to the arguments of Persons he had long before given a direct and positive answer. When he joined the expeditions of 1596 and 1597 against the Spaniards he signified that he was prepared to shed his blood for a Protestant Queen against her Catholic enemies.

In the end Donne's rejection of the Jesuits was far more vehement than his rejection of Catholicism. In spite of the violence of his polemical attacks on the Jesuits, he never lost sympathy for those Catholics who wanted to preserve both their religion and their patriotism. He understood too well the personal dissatisfaction and emotional conflict that resulted from leaving them unreconciled, and he wrote *Pseudo-Martyr* to persuade 'some irresolved and

[1] See the letter to Sir Henry Goodere, Gosse, *Life and Letters of Donne*, I, 225.

undetermined persons' how they could make a reconciliation. In a sense Donne is only attempting a restatement, in terms of altered circumstances, of the issues that Southwell had stated nearly twenty years before.

Yet in another, and more real, sense *Pseudo-Martyr* marks the final rejection of an ideal of Donne's youth, and one which Southwell, more than any of his co-religionists except perhaps Edmund Campion, had personified. Donne's 'first breeding and conversation' had been with 'men of suppressed and afflicted Religion, accustomed to the despite of death, and hungry of an imagin'd Martyrdome', and Southwell's *Supplication* is permeated with this hunger for martyrdom. Yet in 1610 Southwell's death was to Donne no real martyrdom, but at most an imagined one, and he wrote *Pseudo-Martyr* to prove that Southwell and many others 'had cast away their blood with a fruitless effusion'. It was not that Donne denied Christianity, nor even the necessity of facing death for Christ, but he had come to feel that the points of difference between the Roman and Reformed churches were insufficient to warrant the shedding of blood. 'The channels of God's mercies', he wrote in a letter of this period, 'run through both fields; they are sister teats of his graces, yet both diseased and infected, but not both alike',[1] and in the *Essays in Divinity* a few years later he repeated:

though we branch out *East* and *West*, that Church [the Roman] concurs with us in the root, and sucks her vegetation from one and the same ground, *Christ Jesus*; who, as it is in the *Canticle*, lies between the brests of his Church, and gives suck on both sides.

The suspended judgement of the *Third Satire* has thus been superseded by a conviction, that, though 'the form of Gods worship, established in the Church of *England*, be more convenient and advantageous then of any other Kingdome, both to provoke and kindle devotion, and also to fix it', the issues between Rome and England were all of 'things not essentiall' to salvation.[2] They justified, therefore, neither persecution nor martyrdom.

[1] Gosse, ii, 78.
[2] *Essays in Divinity*, ed. E. M. Simpson, pp. 49–51.

THE END

Date Due

PRINTED IN U. S. A.